MW00626366

PINE NUTS

Recollections of Summers
at Interlochen

THOM FEILD

TFD LLC / SEATTLE

Interlochen is a registered trademark of Interlochen Center for the Arts.
Book design/illustration: Thom Feild Design LLC

ISBN 0-9786677-0-0
1.   Interlochen Arts Camp (Michigan) I. Title.
ddc21 – 792.028

For more information, visit
www.pinenutsthebook.com

Printed in Michigan,
United States of America

To all those *who listened to their kids dreaming of making a life in the arts that begins with one summer of magic. And most of all, for my parents, who always listened,* got it, *no questions asked.*

CONTENTS

To begin with, Interlochen wasn't a typical summer camp. There were no rows of pitched tents or horses (or playing of horseshoes) or youths lazing around with fishing poles by a lake. A true American character named Joseph Maddy dreamed up the idea for the camp, originally called the National High School Orchestra Camp, and it opened in the woods of northern Michigan a year before the 1929 stock market crash, at a time when camps were mostly for health and recreation or Boy Scouting. Very soon after being established, the camp expanded its offerings so that music was joined by theatre, dance, and art. A brochure from the 1960s puts things in sanitary, truculent terms:

Wholesome outdoor life with excellent food, regular hours, healthful recreation, superior instruction and carefully supervised living and learning conditions make Interlochen the ideal environment in which to develop physically, mentally and morally.

The description makes it sound like a normal, ordinary camp. Or maybe a nudist colony with a socialist bent tucked into secluded woods. The noteworthy phrase in the camp description is "carefully supervised living and learning conditions." Other than the arts activity going on everywhere, rules, order, and structure were the most prominent aspects of Interlochen. And the most source of fun for its followers.

The grounds and outlay are considerable—twelve hundred acres, bordering two lakes, dotted with dozens of cabins, classrooms, practice buildings, studios, and performing spaces. In any given summer, more than two thousand people are studying, teaching, performing, counseling. Students as young as eight attend, but most are high school kids from every state and forty countries.

During my summers there as a camper, and later as a staff member, the whole strictitarian aspect of Interlochen made it seem something like a severe English prep school frozen in the 1920s or '30s. Campers and staff devised various nicknames for it, including Nazi Boot Camp (rules and control at every step) and National Neuter Camp (no time for anything but practice for American's future artists). Yet, oddly enough, the names were more affectionate than vicious or resentful.

Fighting against camp's control was pointless, so developing a survivalist's dark sense of humor was something that camp's inhabitants—campers and staff alike—did quickly and with a certain amount of conspiratorial glee. When it comes down to it, discipline is a handy thing to get used to if you're going to become a musician or any type of artist. So in that sense, the endless rules and structure made sense—it was an early kick-butt reality check for young artist wannabes, conveying how arduously and perpetually artists have to work at their craft. In some ways this was apparent to arriving campers right away, what with the brightest and best all in one place, creating a truly frightening level of competition.

IF INTERLOCHEN HAD BEEN a normal camp, I surely wouldn't have gotten so worked up to go there for two summers in the mid-'60s when I was fifteen and sixteen. I just wasn't a joiner; no Boy Scouts, school clubs, or team sports, and definitely no student government for me. The whole concept of camp seemed utterly juvenile and a waste of time. Summer camp was what dumb kids did or something parents thought of to take time off from their children, at least for part of the summer.

Even though I was totally (and happily) invisible at high school, I was very busy at a full-time career in the theatre. My secret, exciting other life.

From the time I was eleven until I headed to college at eighteen, I moved along on my own little path of fire—destined, I was sure, to become the next important force of Broadway. I organized all the kids I knew who were keen on the idea of being in a show and produced fourteen plays, mostly in the summers and occasionally during the school year. Fifty or sixty kids bit the bullet. We rehearsed the plays, created sets and costumes, borrowed pianos, harpsichords, or follow spots, and secured auditoriums. Everyone chipped in loan-shares so we could rent equipment, buy materials, and pay for royalties.

It was a shoebox version of the adult world of show biz, with production schedules, actors' and production photos, press releases, and even reviews and articles about us in the *Washington Post* and *Washington Star* newspapers. When I look back, it strikes me how much time and effort went into the publicity and printing processes—beginning with cutting mimeograph stencils on manual typewriters in order to print up scripts. Later there were those funny-smelling purple ditto copies, old-fashioned letterpress-printed tickets (and ticket envelopes with sponsored advertising on them) and, particularly, screen printing of posters—a rite of passage for everyone, it seemed, actors included.

My role was producer, fund-raiser, director, composer, and designer. It was strictly Parents Keep Out, not without a few tangles with unreasonable curfews and other obstacles. I remember adults poking me at my parents' cocktail parties and saying, "Hey there, son, you look like you're headed to become the next David Merrick!"

But David Merrick was only a producer. I wanted to direct, design the look of everything, and be the one to think up the grand concepts that would come off almost as elaborately as I'd sketched out and hoped for.

In looking back at these enterprising, whirling-dervish days, I realize that I was completely fearless. Sometimes we made use of ready-made scripts (Albee, Ionesco, Orwell), but more often I adapted our favorite books into plays, and in doing so corresponded with Ogden Nash, Harold Arlen, and James Thurber's widow, Helen. I got in touch with Martin

Gardner, author of *The Annotated Alice,* securing permission for us to present *Alice in Wonderland* and a dramatization of his book in side-by-side versions. Anything was game, and everything was "why not?"—so that our little gang of Mickeys and Judys could put on our extravaganzas.

Putting on these shows gave me everything high school couldn't. Somehow we never lost any money, and forming lifelong friendships was the added gain from the toils, heartache, and teenage brush with greasepaint. With their optimism and natural adrenalin, there is nothing that high school kids can't do, provided they have access to sufficient amounts of junk food and the nonstop mantra of singable Broadway cast albums (*Sweet Charity, Man of La Mancha,* and—for some reason—the flop musical version of *The Secret Life of Walter Mitty*).

Piano lessons still figured in there in the background, as well as a nagging notion of becoming a composer or musical performer. In the early '60s, junior high school presented us with something called the Kuder Preference Record to get us thinking about career ideas or notions of particular college majors. The test was made up of a series of clumsy, not terribly well-disguised questions.

Would you rather:

a. Plant something in a flowerpot?

b. Figure out how to mass-produce flowerpots?

c. Distribute potted flowers to the elderly or sick?

d. Draw a picture of a flowerpot?

My Kuder test came up 100 percent artistic and 99 percent musical. Choosing a direction in my life was not going to be the problem. Finding enough time in the day without skipping out of school was more my concern. Piano teachers and parents always seemed ready with questions like "What about becoming a concert pianist? Or a jazz musician like Dave Brubeck?" Not as many parents were willing to suggest a life in show biz, say in theatre or the movies. Luckily, my parents thought all the stuff I was into was great. I was on my way, and I could hardly wait.

In short, I was the prototypical precocious teenager destined to go to Interlochen, even though it wouldn't be to pursue the goal that most starstruck kids fixate upon: becoming an actor. As far as acting goes, I can recall only two appearances onstage, neither of which seemed to charm me into wanting more time in the spotlight.

My acting debut came in third grade, when I was growing up in Detroit. I was chosen to play the red squirrel in *Hansel and Gretel*. The teacher-director of the school holiday play explained in very serious tones that despite the fact that this was not a speaking role, I was the critical figure in the plotline. In the Winterhalter Elementary version, the bread crumbs Gretel had scattered when the two children went into the forest were still part of the story, but at the end, it was my job as the smart red squirrel to cheerfully lead the two back home to safety once the witch was burned in her own furnace (performed, strangely, to the singing of "Ding Dong, the Witch Is Dead" from *The Wizard of Oz*).

I was a chipper little redheaded boy with a winning come-hither gesture wearing a rust-colored corduroy squirrel costume that my mom had slaved to create from a Butterick pattern, a snug, comfy affair with mitten paws and a bulky tail stuffed with shredded foam rubber and crumpled-up pages of the *Detroit Free Press*. The costume also marked the beginning of my close relationship with corduroy, which was to continue well into my teens and beyond.

Naturally, throughout the years following this auspicious debut, I've had to backpedal quite a bit about my "important" acting role, explaining exactly who the red squirrel was in the context of the generally accepted version of the fairy tale. But no matter: my acting was just an experiment, a diversion. My sights were set on becoming the youngest Franco Zeffirelli ever.

So off I went to Interlochen in 1965 and 1966 for two exciting, dramatic, intense summers of theatre, music, radio, and a chance to do exactly what I was already doing, but in a much fuller, preprofessional way. And to do it all alongside a lot of seriously talented other kids my own age.

IN 1972 I RETURNED TO CAMP as a staff member in the theatre arts department, and that was the best Interlochen summer of all. Gone was the anxiety of youth, and before me was the new freedom of finally being out of school and living in the real arts world that still beckoned with a certain amount of glitter and intrigue.

I'd left Pittsburgh and art school with impossibly grandiose career plans, and the bubble hadn't burst yet. For half of my college years I studied set and costume design, and eventually I finished up in painting/fine arts. You'd think I would have narrowed my focus after getting a degree in painting, but some part of me thought that keeping all my options open wasn't such a terrible idea.

Of course, there was the nasty business of how I would actually make a living and who would be my first employer. After all, it wasn't as if I had an agent and a gallery lined up to represent me. Earning a B.F.A. in painting is a bit like getting a B.A. in English—it's a springboard to something (else). Kids take quite a range of non-sequitur jobs after finishing art school: waiter, child care worker, and any job that's remotely visual—like color tile specialist or store-window-display designer.

And so I delayed the downer of the first crummy job after college by deciding to go back to work at Interlochen, since it still held fond memories. I couldn't resist. At times I've made quick, offhand decisions that turned out to be just right, and this was certainly one of them.

The two vivid high school summers and the return as staff at the close of college were complementary bookends of experience, the child and adult versions of the same place, just in slightly different time zones. But the only way I can re-create my own distilled essence of Interlochen is to tell it week by week, that season on staff in the early 1970s.

Re-sounding the Call

Oh, sound the call to dear old Interlochen!
Land of the stately pine.
Where stalwart hands and loyal ever greet you.
Faithful for Auld Lang Syne.

Old friends you'll meet,
New ones you'll greet,
A welcome you'll ever find.
So, sound the call to dear old Interlochen!
Shrine of the muse divine.

— T. Henry Francis, "Sound the Call (Interlochen Bowl March)"

SO HERE I WAS AGAIN, in June 1972, a returning veteran of Interlochen, looking forward to the camp rituals and routines, seeing how new (or threadbare) my camp-provided uniforms were going to be. I wondered what major concerts and performances would be in the lineup; would Van Cliburn appear again and play the Tchaikovsky First or Rach Three? Which plays, musicals, operettas were on the schedule? And once again I had the funny sensation that no one had actually gone home, that the archetypal Interlochen cast of characters had been merely resting in pleasant cold storage—waiting to be reactivated, same place, same faces, the following year, continuing exactly where they left off.

On the day before camp began, thousands of kids arrived by plane, bus, and car within a twenty-four-hour period, creating an exhilarating, movielike scene of screams, reunions, and frenetic anticipation. Student musicians practiced scales and silent sight reading in their family cars on the way to camp in preparation for the auditions, which would place them in different ensembles. Actors warmed up with vocal exercises to try out for coveted roles; dancers stretched and preened, readying themselves to audition for ballets and modern dance pieces.

Piled high at the center of camp and in dusty patches in front of cabins were umpteen metal campers' footlockers with Interlochen stickers plastered on them, shipped by a now long-defunct company called Railway Express Agency. (REA wasn't ground shipping—it was tortoise, with four to six weeks or more of delivery time.) The trunks contained red V-neck sweaters, raincoats and rubbers, Keds tennis shoes; green wool camp blankets; pitch pipes, pocket metronomes, pointe shoes and leotards; *Elson's Pocket Music Dictionary*, Stanislavski's *An Actor*

Prepares, Moss Hart's *Act One*; sheet music and scripts, artist sketchbooks, mosquito repellent, flashlights, monophonic transistor radios with single earpieces, Vanilla Wafers metal tins containing Mom's homemade cookies, and stationery on which to write letters home.

Even as staff and veteran, I needed the big white foldout camp map. Camp buildings were variously labeled as huts, shells, and bowls, or simply coded with letters and numbers. There were music-  teacher studio cabins, brass instrument storage, the harp hut, instrument repair, a stage scenery warehouse, two radio station facilities, costume shops, a dance studio perched above the edge of one of two lakes, music and academic libraries, laundries—an endless array of buildings designed to cope with and contain everything that would go on at full tilt during the next eight weeks.

Music practice booths—fourteen to a building, seven on either side—were woven throughout the landscape of camp like strands of DNA. The ones with pianos mostly had wretched spinets with half a dozen nonworking keys. At one point camp had over a hundred pianos, so keeping them all tuned, especially in summer, was an impossibility. Baldwin supplied many of them, and rumor had it they'd resell some at summer's end with stickers proclaiming, "The keys of this piano were touched by a gifted youth of Interlochen."

A spin on camp's tagline, "Guiding America's Gifted Youth."

On this, my first afternoon back at camp, I stepped into one of the booths without thinking, recalling immediately my quest as a pianist-camper to nab one of the better instruments to practice on. One week into the summer, any pianist would know exactly where the good pianos were to be found. The little room smelled of damp wood, and the floor was dusted with dirt from the footpaths. Cobwebs sagged on the windows. An old soda cup stood sadly on the floor in the corner of the room, and an abandoned copy of violin exercises rested on a black metal music stand. A still life about to shake and rattle back into motion.

The proximity of so many booths in a single practice building always made me think of the Tin Pan Alley songwriters of the '20s and '30s, jammed into tight cubicles, driven to turn out hit tunes. Yet these little studios ended up harboring fond memories for so many, in later years. Each one was a camper's own little practice studio, far better than the damp rec room back home.

Walking anywhere on campus, especially in those first few days, I heard the ferocious poundings of the keyboard portions of piano concertos, the blended cacophony of six or seven within yards of each other, while a passage from the Mozart French horn concerto occasionally rose above the demonic keyboards. Death-defying playing, all very sobering for the average piano student hugging a copy of Bach's two-part inventions.

Although a staff member or student could come to

camp solely for dance, theatre, or art, the constant barrage of music everywhere was still the canvas, the soundtrack, setting the mood of each day in a thrilling way. If you stood at the center of camp, you would always be within earshot of two or more large ensembles playing full tilt, musical pieces blending and overlapping like the key-change pyrotechnics of a Richard Strauss opera. The effect resembled a sort of brilliantly colored, alcohol-laden sound cocktail. The swell of music always seemed to work its magic on visitors, too, the moment they walked into the center of camp.

Automatically, I found myself slipping back into camp mode—rules, mottos, jargon, and all. A new arrival, camper or staff, quickly learned that deviating from any policy—on uniforms, for example—meant that everyone around you would pounce immediately with semiserious censure: Camp Frowns. (Sadly or not, there was no Camp Smiles to counterbalance.) You wouldn't necessarily be punished, but you would suffer plenty of ridicule from all quarters.

Camp embraced various slogans to keep things orderly and tuned to its own needs. My friend Jonathan reminded me years later of one motto, "In the arts there are no enemies!," which we found as funny as it was untrue. There was also "Be at the right place at the right time," which in camper days my friend Matthew found vaguely fascistic and sadly at odds with the joy that was supposed to be part of pursuing the arts. I couldn't help thinking that this latter slogan was used at boys' military schools to better effect.

At camp, every concert performance was followed by a little encore-coda called the Interlochen Theme—a lush, pastoral snippet bequeathed by Howard Hansen from his Second Symphony (the "Romantic"). The rule, which you learned quickly, was that the Theme was always followed with silence. Anyone who clapped, usually a tourist or visiting parent, was *shhhh*ed vigorously. Applause was an insult to the shrine. It was always a bit of fun to be on the home team, providing the reminder, casting the aspersions.

THE FIRST FEW DAYS of settling in were atypical because everything was on the verge and about to explode, but the cannon hadn't sounded yet. We staff were about to begin the process of figuring out how to organize and pull off five high school theatre productions in eight weeks with as few snags as possible and in the most professional way the campers could manage. It took six-day weeks and five-hour class days, with nonstop rehearsals and preparation, to make it all happen. There were no classes on Sundays; instead there were a dozen or more performances, very much like the real, grown-up worlds of music, theatre, and dance.

Although I knew almost no one else on staff by the time I came back for this encore summer, I was familiar with the culture, the rules of the game, and the pace of what was to come. I knew that the next eight weeks were going to be amusing, at the very least.

That summer I was the theatre arts department production manager, which meant I was the prop maker and also responsible for teaching stage-managing to High School Drama students who had an interest in stagecraft—or who might be recruited to help run the shows. Over the years, the head of the theatre department had developed a good sense of how to assemble each summer's staff, drawing on fellow college professors and their undergrad drama students.

New or returning, everyone looked forward to an invigorating, fast-clip summer in a place where the weather was agreeable and the setting glorious. Northern Michigan might have been an unfamiliar gamble for the youngest new recruits, but they lucked out. And we all found, as the summer rolled along, that high school students at this deeper end of the talent pool were great fun to work with as well as receptive sponges for what we might pass along.

On my first day, before checking in at the theatre, I slinked through the main part of the campus to get a feel for everything, take in the mood, and listen for snippets of frenetic reunions. By habit, I walked up to glance at two of the most vital, popular bulletin boards at the center of camp. One was an events board on which programs for each day's performances, recitals, and events would be posted. This day, before the official opening, was the only day of the summer when the board didn't have five to ten detailed programs covering its surface.

I moved on to the large, folksy, pine-framed map that was updated each summer to reflect where campers hailed from. Although all camp members wore a name badge that included their hometown, it was fascinating to see a visual representation of the states populated with colored map pins, from the tiniest towns in North Dakota to the major metros of the East Coast to the extra off-map pins for Puerto Rico,

France, or Scandinavia. Just as in my camper days, a little congregation stood in front of it, pointing and conversing.

"Where you guys from?" I asked three campers. A switch went off inside me; it felt new and a little odd to step into the non-camper role. I was taller, older, but I certainly didn't feel like a camp official. And there was something comforting in being only four years older than the oldest high school camper.

There was a pause. The two preteen girls looked a bit embarrassed, frozen by my question. The older high school boy spoke up.

"I'm from western Massachusetts. Pittsfield. It's not a very latch town."

"You talk funny! What kind of accent is *that*?" one of the girls said.

"Yeah," chimed in the other. She giggled. "What is a…latch town?"

"LATCH, not small," answered the boy, looking wearily familiar with these jabs at his New England accent.

"Anyway, I'm from Shaker Heights, Ohio. I'm studying flute," the first girl piped up, suddenly much more confident.

"And I'm from Erie, Pennsylvania," added the other. "I'm really here for dance—ballet and stuff. But I'm taking art, too."

The two of them crunched at their soft ice cream cones and quickly darted away toward a bunch of other girls their age. The boy continued to study the map, leaning in for a closer look, when a high school girl joined us at the map.

"Hi, Jeff. How's it going?" she asked.

"Oh, hi, Gwen. Fine. Things are good. Good," answered the boy. He looked happy to see her; I guessed the two were both musicians, played different instruments, and weren't direct competitors.

"How was your school year? You practicing like crazy for auditions?" she asked.

"Well, yeah. Same as last year. I'm busting to make World Youth this year. I really worked hard, improved a lot over the winter."

"Mmm," she nodded. She said nothing for a moment or two and just kept nodding her head, then added, "Such a big deal. I mean—performing in all the broadcasts is neat. It's always kinda weird, getting in, you know?" Her voice changed, taking on a low, nasal quality as she leaned into the map and added, "Seems like you either hafta be first chair or have wild hair."

The boy stared at her, smirked, and they both burst out laughing.

I couldn't help snickering along softly. The two campers had hit on an interesting point, and the laughs confirmed it. It was clear that the two had been coming to camp for a few years. The Interlochen World Youth Symphony Orchestra was considered the best ensemble of the two orchestras and two bands formed each summer. Camper musicians got in if they were tops, but they also got in if they were from another country and could play reasonably well. At least, that was campers' take on it.

From the very beginning, camp cofounder Joseph Maddy

was a smart promoter, especially when it came to his knack for arranging radio broadcasts. The more international and exciting the Interlochen image, the more students and educators (and donors) would continue to flock there, year after year. Grumbling in the student ranks wasn't that common; everyone got to perform—and perform a great deal—in eight weeks' time.

Later that afternoon we opened Grunow Theatre and got busy cleaning, preparing everything so the productions could get rolling. So far I'd met the set designer and the shop assistants. Around the theatre and in the scene shop, doors and windows were hammered open, and buckets of cleanser were scattered about. The sounds were of sweeping, spray hoses, laughter, and each of the play directors shuffling into the drama office for their big theatrical hellos and welcome-backs. The theatre's basement costume shop still smelled dank and musty and felt dark and tomblike, in sharp contrast to the bustling beehive it would become a day or two later.

My first job was repainting the theatre's wood trim. With my brush and bucket of brown paint in hand, I was just turning the corner toward the back of the building when a short, compact, tanned and smiling man came toward me carrying several Fresnel stage lights, with heavy electrical cables strung over one shoulder.

"Hi. You're the lighting guy, right?" I said.

"Yeah. I'm Bob, you're...ah, Thom?" he answered.

"Right. Nice to meet you. Well, so, how's it all looking?"

"Good. It'll be fine. I've seen worse!" Bob chuckled

softly. He put the lights down on the ground in order to talk. A sociable sign, I thought.

"I just hope they're not all little Richard Burtons and Elizabeth Taylors in the bunch," I said, "and we get a few kids who want to run the light boards and move scenery,"

"Rrright," answered Bob, getting where I was going.

"I guess we'll just have to remind some of them that doing lights, props, and stage managing means a life of glamour and travel. Like being in a rock band. And that being backstage or in the booth is where the real power is."

Bob's thick walrus mustache gave way to a pretty good-sized Cheshire cat grin. "Ya got that right!" Both of us laughed.

Whew, I thought; I could see that Bob and I were going to get along fine, which was a good thing, considering what summer always had in store—backstage power failures, July heat waves, and bats terrorizing actors in their dressing rooms, among other things.

"We're all supposed to head out to the warehouse later on to do a major clean-out. See what there is," I said. "I hear there's quite a bit of stuff piled up from some of the winter academy productions."

"Right..." Bob nodded, smiling.

"So were you on staff last summer?"

"No, no...I kinda got persuaded into coming up this summer with a bunch of us from San Diego State. Were you here last summer?"

"No—but I was here as a high school camper for two summers," I answered, widening my eyes and adding with emphasis, "... in *drama*! Funnily enough—painting scenery and making props, the techie kid heading to drama school to study set design. So it can't have been that bad—I'm back!"

"Huh...cool," Bob said, looking sort of impressed and surprised. "Well, seems like a good group. We just have to get that first show up pretty quick."

"Yup," I nodded. "I should let you hang lights, then." I poked my brush around in the can to freshen up the paint, then turned around to see that a tiny pixie of a woman had come bounding up behind me.

"B-o-b...!" she said, grinning.

"Hey, Mary. You're here already. You met Thom?" Bob said.

"Hi, Thom. You've got a paint bucket—that's a good sign!" Mary smiled. She had short blond hair pulled back under a paint-splattered red bandana. Her bright blue eyes were open wide and intensely focused on me, with laugh lines digging firmly into her freckled tan. She was somewhere in her late thirties, with a sort of gleeful, almost giddy energy that was infectious. She was smiling so hard, it was as if she were waiting for me to deliver a knockout punch line.

"Yeah, and you've got on quite a war-veteran paint-splattered shirt," I said. "And this is only the first day...or are we doing a Jackson Pollock set, and you just couldn't wait to get started?"

Mary burst out in wonderful explosive laughter. I hadn't said anything that funny, I thought, but it seemed her way to start a friendship and waste no time.

"Oh, this is from two summers ago!" she said. "I hope you've met Susie, another of us from San Diego?"

"Mmm, not yet. Is she working in the scene shop too?" I asked.

Mary burst out laughing again, even giddier than before. "Costumes. She'll be entertaining us all summer, fershure, you'll see. Well... great to meet you, Thom. I need to go open a bunch more cans of black casein, which froze and separated during the winter." She rolled her eyes. "A pretty familiar state of things—in other words, we're right on schedule!"

She trotted off, giggling, as we all forged ahead on our tasks. It was a perfect sunny day to be outdoors hauling back and forth corroded, useful junk and painted flats, the raw ingredients of illusion. All of us happily thrusting our hands into paint and sawdust in order for the games to begin.

THE FOLLOWING DAY it was time for the all-camp opening assembly. In the early days of Interlochen, this was held in the camp's original amphitheater—the rustic Interlochen Bowl, which was log-trimmed or pine-paneled on every conceivable surface. Its stage was almost a barn, with one side open; the audience area was a raked, powder-dry dirt slope with wire-and-wood-slat park benches that were

never quite securely footed to much of anything. Dozens of trees, some with electric tin lanterns hanging from them, grew up amid the benches, so you had to pick your seats carefully to ensure a clear view of the stage.

But these days the opening assembly was held in the more modern Kresge Auditorium, a four-thousand-seat covered amphitheater that looked something like a giant concrete-and-steel Timex watch box with a wood-shingled roof. Both the Bowl and Kresge were situated with their stages perched on the edge of Lake Wahbekanetta. At the rear of Kresge's stage was an expanse of five glass-windowed archways looking out on the lake, which formed a dreamy backdrop to the lush string passages of the *Romeo and Juliet Fantasy Overture* or Tchaikovsky's Fourth Symphony—two pieces that showed up over the course of the summer with unfailing regularity, by the composer who was surely the most popular with the youngest campers.

I slipped into an aisle seat, taking in the atmosphere of frenetic anticipation. Everyone was talking, laughing, bristling; a measurable electricity was in the air. Moments before the ceremony began, a noiseless, calming lake breeze glided in across the audience. The contrast between such calm and the dramatic tension was part of the pleasure and odd thrill I felt in that moment, sitting and waiting for the music and spirit about to burst forth.

The opening ceremony began with a wallop: three thousand campers and staff launched into singing the camp song, "Sound the Call," at the top of their lungs. Following the singing blowout were the familiar, inclusive rituals of campers rising and yelling as each of their fifty states and forty-odd countries were called out; more spirit songs and cheers; and rah-rah welcome speeches about what a great summer it was going to be. Truly preaching to the choir, since everyone was hyperenthusiastic, almost to the point of political-campaign fervor.

Once again I was swept into it, this perennial Interlochen show on display, one in a massive assemblage of kids who felt like misfits in their own schools at home but who, when they came to a haven like this, were spring-loaded to come alive for a brief eight weeks in the company of so many more of their own kind.

Twenty minutes into the ceremonies the Junior girls, the youngest girl campers, did their reworded rendition of "The Candy Man," a song popularized that year by Sammy Davis Jr. The girls leapt up from their seats, looking like tiny dolls in matching outfits—grinning, shout-singing, their voices so piercing and high that everyone had to turn to face these jumping-bean cheerleaders of camp spirit:

Who's got the stuff that brings the camp a big smile,
Junior Girrrrrls!

A few rows in front of me were Mary and a young, curvaceous woman with long, straight red hair. They both turned around suddenly, looking in my direction, and all of us burst out laughing, exchanging eye rolls at this out-and-out cornfest of little Whoville voices. The redhead was the Susie I'd heard about, of course. She and I were to become friends instantly and, with Bob, would comprise a fiercely cavorting trio for the weeks that followed.

Escape Velocity

TIME WAS GOING ZIP ZIP ALREADY. So much happening all at once—classes, rehearsals, costumes and scenery under construction, and theatre productions in motion. At Interlochen, there were so many performances all going on simultaneously each day that the printed programs indicated the stats: "This is the ninety-sixth performance of the forty-fifth season." All told, there would be 350 to 400 performances. In addition, camp photographed every ensemble and major event, and recorded them too, so campers could obtain tapes later on.

That summer the theatre department numbered about twenty faculty and staff, overseeing drama for Juniors (the eight- to twelve-year-olds), Intermediates (junior high age), and high school campers. Most of us were hired to work exclusively with the five high school productions. In addition to the San Diego crew, our group included college professors and students from Milwaukee and Tucson, with a smattering of us East Coasters.

High School Drama was already revving up with its first offering, *The Visit*, a wonderfully grisly play by Friedrich Dürrenmatt. It would be followed by *See How They Run, The Music Man*, *Iolanthe*, and *As You Like It*. The incoming talent level was high, and I didn't envy the directors' task of having to quickly make assessments, cast the productions, and, within the first few days, schedule everything into a tightly packed matrix. Some High School Drama majors were strong in both acting and singing, so the theatre department would want to make use of them in a play, a musical comedy, *and* an operetta. One such kid, from my own first camper summer, was Tovah Feldshuh. At fifteen or sixteen, she stood out with star quality and was promptly cast in as many productions as possible. Tovah would later sail on to Broadway and television, nabbing multiple Tony and Emmy nominations.

By week two I'd already been having a ball working every day with Mary and Bob, and I was getting to know the vivacious Susie, who was stranded for the most part among the purring Singers and the sewing circle of the costume shop. I liked being able to do most of the prop construction out-of-doors, camped out on the back steps of the theatre, ideally situated to catch snippets of conversation from the open windows of both the theatre office and the costume shop. There was piano music coming from a teacher's studio cabin nearby, and a postcard view of one of the two lakes.

Work was fun; life was good.

I was sitting on the sun-bleached wooden steps removing labels from old, shapely beer bottles to transform them into period props when Susie appeared, galloping up the ramp that led from Costumes to ground level, her arms over her head in a cartoon showgirl pose, belting out what sounded like a Rodgers and Hart song. A couple of actor-campers sitting on the grass looked up suddenly, realizing it was that redhead from the costume shop—the seamstress who wasn't as serious as the others working there.

"Hey, you!" I beamed.

"Why, yes, it's *me*, isn't it!" Susie exclaimed in a high, fluted voice, quickly launching into song. "I'm a sentimental sap, that's all.... what's the use of trying not to fall?..."

"Susie, you always burst into song whenever I see you. I'm never sure if you're turning into one of the campers or if that's the real you," I said, laughing before I could finish.

"Thom—*it's the real me*," Susie said in a firm Helen of Troy voice, grinning.

"Stopped downstairs earlier to pick up my mail, but you weren't around," I said in a mock whine.

"Oh, I was probably up in the girls' dressing room. They're rehearsing with practice muslin skirts for *The Visit* today," she said. "I needed to get out of there for a few minutes. It's getting too costume girl–tense downstairs with all the final fittings before dress/tech."

"And how are the prima dons and donnas doing?" I said.

"Honestly, they are so funny, some of them. I mean..."

She stopped, remembering to lower her voice, her eyebrows and face distorted as if in pain. "It's not just the girls. One boy slips down several times a day and asks when will we be ready for his next fitting. He says he needs to see his costume to help him get into character—'course, I think he is really just hoping that his suit is flattering enough!"

"Ha, right. But think about it. It's pretty different from doing plays back in his high school," I suggested.

"You're right. Instead of Mom doing their costume or going to Goodwill," she mused, "here there is a real costume designer and all these assistants to fuss over them. Clare is great with them."

"Guess you heard—we're using 'George Spelvin' in the printed program for the coffin body and the station master's voice."

"What?" Susie said.

"You know—the old theatre tradition of using 'George Spelvin' in the credits whenever there is a corpse or a unseen voice?" I said.

"Right...so...?" Susie looked stumped.

"The parts seemed too puny to be given to a camper. But the kids had no idea and were fascinated to find out who Spelvin was, so Don had to explain it all."

"So the corpse is camp staff. Nice."

"Ha. Yeah," I shrugged.

By this time, seven or eight kids were hanging out behind the theatre. All had their noses buried in wrinkled, orange paper–covered Samuel French scripts, and a few were quizzing each other, running lines.

"Look at them. They're so intense," said Susie, smiling.

"I know, I know," I answered.

"I guess some of the kids' parents show up at camp when their shows go on, right?" Susie ventured.

"Some do. It's funny, though," I added. "You never hear them worrying or talking about that. It's like their mission is to prove to the directors and to each other that they can do it."

"They're already stepping off from the high school play thing at home, right," Susie said, pausing to think about it for another moment.

"Catch you toward dinner?"

"Uh-huh. I see Clare waving at me anyway. I better run," said Susie, rushing her petite, buxom costume-lady self back to the den of pin cushions and shears.

Susie was right about one thing. Claremarie, the head costumer that summer, was a solid find in the group. She was a Rubenesque, cheery mother figure to all, a comedienne blend of Jo Anne Worley and Nanette Fabray and a mainstay of the Milwaukee contingent.

Clare and I made more trips to town than the others in order to secure fabric and props and bring back special food requests. Town was Traverse City, always referred to as T.C. Hauling fifteen miles or so in order to get there was rare for campers and infrequent for staff, who were usually entangled in long days of camp duties.

Those trips typically included our bringing back heaps of ever-abundant, massively plump sweet dark cherries, and occasionally really touristy things like cherry ice cream or pink fudge. Traverse City considers itself the cherry capital of the world, with a national cherry festival in July and the Cherry City Airport year-round.

By the end of the second week, Bob and Susie and I had taken a good look at most of the drama students, picking the winners, the whiners, and the ones that were younger iterations of ourselves. Although Susie and I were getting chummy, I was also starting to be taken under Mary's wing—which kept things interesting. Mary had been coming to Interlochen long enough to have seen every angle. Yet her overall attitude combined jaded familiarity with genuine anticipation as to what new twists and people might be added to that summer's mix.

On this particular day, Mary and the scene shop crew were all out-of-doors either painting, gluing, or "aging" things, so it was easy for the two of us to distract one another with jokes and banter. I walked over to her, struck a stiff, disapproving pose, and launched into my impression of the musical's choreographer, Adrianne. I made my eyes bulge out, mimed hiding a cigarette, looked very dissatisfied, shifted my weight onto one leg, and muttered, "It's o—kay. I mean, it *might* be okay. We're not all going to be Fosse dancers here. But I'd really like a lot more finite energy and sizzle in those moves—we're talking the High School Drama musical here, the Main Event of the summer." A pause for effect, then: "I'm just not *seeing* it yet."

"*Wicked*, Thom!" exclaimed Mary, exploding with the contagious laughter that was already her trademark (along with "fershure"—something I figured must be a California thing, since camp was the first time I'd encountered it).

I felt a little guilty. The choreographer, whom the High School Drama majors all called Miss Adrianne, was just the sort of intense teacher/former dancer that the kids adored and worked their asses off for. She and the musical theatre–loving students spent all winter long dreaming of summer at Interlochen, and they would, once more, pull off one monster of a musical in a matter of four weeks.

THE FIRST PERFORMANCE of *The Visit* went well— the kids had been pros, as expected, and we were off to a fine start. To celebrate, Susie and I had rallied some of the livelier staff to head into town afterward for drinks and dancing. I wasn't even sure that counselors managed to do things like that. It all seemed so racy and adult, perhaps because most of our days were being spent with teenagers.

After the performance I milled around on the back steps of the theatre, trying to figure out where our group was. Suddenly, in the moonlight, a figure came flying at me like a caped Zorro. It was Susie. She had on a full-length emerald green velveteen coat and a floppy hat. The voluminous getup took me aback at first, since we'd barely seen each other in anything but camp uniforms since the start of summer.

"Let's go! Are you ready or not?" she demanded.

"Almost. Wait. Bob's shutting down the circuit breakers and locking up," I answered, excited that we were finally going to leave camp en masse and be Wild Things. The only thought running through my brain was *It's Susie in her coach-and-four coat.*

"Well, I wish he'd hustle his bustle! Mary's waiting with the car. Clare, Mariann, Gary, and the others have left already. Bill's can't WAIT!"

"I know, *I know*!" I wailed back. We were headed to a lively club in town called Bill's Dills, which had live music and was the draw that summer.

At 10 p.m. it was chilly, one of the exhilarating pleasures of Michigan summers—the dry day's heat could suddenly fade into a cool night in the 60s or even the 50s. The Norway pines seemed to give off more scent at that hour. An über-camp feeling charged up the night as a silent spray of diamonds twinkled down on us from a sky of deep Prussian jeweler's velvet: quintessential northern Michigan.

Our driver-to-be, Mary, was the classic VW Beetle person—hippie heritage, California dreamin', free-wheelin' and all. Finally she pulled around to the theatre, we piled into her worn Bug with its comforting, unmistakable musty VW smell, and off to town we went.

The club was rollicking, at peak, and seemed poised for us to arrive. We hit the dance floor and acted out in the way that theatre people often do—with louder laughs, bigger gestures, and wilder dance moves. Before long a fair number of people seemed to be looking at us with wide-eyed expressions that said, "Who the *heck* are these loons?"

At one point someone asked us where we were from. I told them we were from "the music camp"—giving in to the general impression people always seemed to have, that Interlochen was only for music.

"I teach bassoon," I said, quickly drawing a long, bookish face and putting down my beer bottle. "And she," I pointed to Susie, "teaches harp. The beautiful long hair, you know, always part of the romantic harp-playing tradition."

Susie smirked, unable to suppress a high-pitched giggle, then shoved Bob in the side of his ribs. I could only go on with the charade.

"Bob teaches saxophone," I continued, gesturing like a tour guide. "And Mary, there, teaches sailing and works part-time at the infirmary."

By this time all four of us were laughing uncontrollably, and the revelers listening to us were looking uneasy and more than a little dubious.

"Naw, I'm just fooling you. I'm sorry," I confessed. "We're from the camp, but actually we all work in the theatre department."

One of the listeners, a sturdy-looking man with sandy blond hair and Wellington boots, smiled uncertainly and nodded, no doubt thinking that none of us were employed at any kind of camp at all. He then said cheerfully, "Well, you sure are great dancers, anyway!" And the rest of his group promptly moved back into the thick of the Saturday night mayhem.

Short of tap dancing on the tables, we let it all out in our celebratory escape from Camp Scrutiny. We were blowing off steam for ourselves as well as for the poor little campers stuck behind in their bunks, lights out hours ago. We drank a lot of beer, then danced it all off; I ate huge amounts of French fries and batter-fried perch. It was perfectly clear that I was one of a lucky pack who would be keen on keeping things at a marvelous, magical high for the rest of the summer.

In the Corduroy Groove

THE PRESSURE WAS ON. With four more productions in rehearsal, the theatre arts department seemed to function at college level and at summer stock's manic pace. The concerto auditions, open to audiences in various performing spaces, were also in full swing. It's quite something to see not one twelve-year-old but dozens of them race their way through treacherous piano concertos in hopes of performing them later in the summer with a full orchestra. Each summer between 125 and 150 kids would audition, and just twenty-five would win the privilege of performing with an orchestra.

They were little music-making dynamos; many would take advantage of the opportunity, at camp, to have an early visit with admissions counselors from Juilliard, Eastman, or Oberlin. I'd done this in my camper days too, even though

I was several years away from applying to schools. But after seeing the level of talent of others my age, and then talking with the music conservatories, I realized I wasn't going to become a concert artist. Camp cleared my vision. I don't remember even feeling jarred or anxious about it. Theatre, art, and design were still calling, and my passion was intact, just focused a bit more.

Those summer interviews for music schools had been held in Interlochen's year-round school building. In the early 1960s, Joseph Maddy had realized his longtime dream of opening an accredited winter/spring-term school for the arts, in addition to the summer camp. The Interlochen Arts Academy, a boarding school, represented a very different version of Interlochen. Only a handful of the campus buildings were winterized, so other new structures had to be built. The student body was around four hundred, and the school was very keen on making sure the academic side was up to snuff. There was always a not-quite-silent cultural divide between summer camp and winter academy, although many campers eventually went on to study at Interlochen year-round.

Just being at camp again brought up a wave of the feelings from my high school summers. I had longed to angle a way into the academy, but I was neither rich enough to afford it nor poor enough to win a scholarship. Back then, in my spare moments I would hang around the academy admissions area, pretending that I was set to attend that fall while poring over brochures as nonchalantly as possible. *There they were*—the lucky ones, sitting in the brochure's orchestra photos with their natty blazers. Not blazers of a garden-variety prep school, but of an *arts* academy. No football games, none of the ordinary high school bullshit. The academy probably didn't even bother with that pretentious Honor Society nonsense, with those candles and rituals of induction that always seemed creepy and more like some quasi-religious ceremony than a way to glorify a school's academic superstars.

It took a few years, but I did eventually get over being an academy wannabe.

DURING MY SUMMER ON STAFF, none of us working in drama ever quite got past the institutional food. Theatre people tend to be gourmets or gourmands; they crave more garlic, more flavor, more of everything. Instead we had to face instant mashed potatoes and stinky, dead canned vegetables. As with many items at camp, the cafeteria trays were well-worn heavy aluminum military surplus—sort of a *Blade Runner* industrial version of a TV dinner tray.

By the end of a day, the staff were as wound up as the campers, and there was the pleasant thought that you weren't sure who you'd dine with, but someone you knew would turn up at your table, along with a new face or two. It was also the best point in the day to get the news and feel the first rumbles about a particular performance or some near-calamity.

The dining hall was as hot as a pressure cooker, so we'd often head out to the back lawn with friends and enjoy dinner on the grass—with a view of the lake and the sound of relaxed laughter rather than the labors of music practice. Just as in my summers as a camper, there'd be a nice lingering lull after the dinner meal, and in another hour I could choose between several performances before turning in.

I remember one particular evening, waiting in the staff line for dinner along with Clare, just taking in the wonderful late-afternoon rays of sun baking my face as the banging of pots and pans and kitchen-sprayer sounds floated out of the dining hall's kitchen windows.

"Hey, Clare...you're here for dinner, not just nibbling on something until 9 or 10 down in the costume shop. Good deal," I began.

"Well, things are reasonably under control today. I deserve it, I think," Clare answered.

"It's nice—we get to eat dinner together, instead of our usual breakfast. Just the two of us," I said. Clare smiled.

Behind her, two staff women, who looked as though they must be counselors, were talking excitedly. They were leaning in closely toward one another; it was obvious that they were discussing something very hush-hush. We were easily able to hear them; Clare and I had similar radars for just this sort of opportunity, and both of us instinctively turned away from the counselors and looked in the opposite direction, while our ears slid upward like motorized antennas.

"So you heard about our little high school incident, then...?" said the taller one. She had a little bit of a toughened look about her. I guessed that she was what some called a "lifer":

someone who has been working at camp for seven or eight years or more.

"No, no, I didn't. *What* happened? Was it this afternoon?" replied the other.

"Just before lunch. Jill, counselor of Cabin Six, found two high school campers carrying on in the woods, not too far from the waterfront," said the taller one.

"You *aren't serious*!?" gasped the other. She tried to lower her voice. "What happened after that?"

"Richardson took them both over to Girls' headquarters, phoned Delucci in High School Boys. Got on the phone with their parents, and they were each packed up and put onto Greyhound buses within the hour," the taller one explained.

"That's *it*, then. Huh," the other gasped, still in disbelief.

"My...word...!" Clare murmured to me, and we exchanged long, stretched face masks of comedy as we turned full-circle away from the counselors to keep from bursting out laughing.

"And it's barely the third week," I whispered back. "Some kids sure move fast!" Clare and I retuned our radars.

"Still, it's surprising, huh?" the taller counselor added. "You have to contain it. And that's what they did. Can't have word of that running around camp."

"Mmm, yeah. Right. Of course," her fellow counselor said, trailing off, already in deep thought. No doubt she was taking in the business of sending home two campers with lightning-quick speed, so as to prevent any campward toxic flow.

Clare and I were quaking, hoping one or the other would think of a conversation topic to keep us from losing it. The seriousness of this sizzling appetizer of overheard news made me think there would really only ever be the four of us at camp who would be in the know—other than the actual parties involved and the staff who took the disciplinary actions, of course. When Susie appeared, Clare and I waved her on ahead to join us in line.

"Hey, Susan Eileen," I called out to her in a brogue.

"Hi, you two. I was wondering who might be up for some meals on metal trays," Susie answered.

"It's so lovely outside, why are we heading into the wretched steamy dining room?" said Clare, half whining, half giggling.

Several places ahead of us in line was a tall man craning his neck to look past everyone into the entrance. He announced to his companions, "Ha—yeah, they're doing the clapping thing again today."

A couple of staffers chuckled; others looked puzzled. Before I could speak, Susie demanded in an alarmed tone, "What? What *is it?* You *know,* don't you?!"

"Mmm...yeah. It's kind of a fun tradition. Sometimes the high school kids do this rhythmic clapping thing when the dinner line is really long."

"No. I have to see this. Let's run over there. Clare can hold our place—right, Clare?"

There was no putting her off—there never was. Years later, at dinner, I would watch Susie order dessert first in a restaurant when something too distracting on the menu caught her eye. So we scooted around to the opposite entrance to the hall, where a long line of high schoolers was winding down a cinderblock corridor and out the back door facing the lake.

There they were, just as I remembered from camper days, girls and some of the boys clapping in loud, rhythmic patterns. Not quite like street kids, not as formal as eurhythmics, the alternating marching-clapping/coordination exercises they still taught in some music conservatories.

"This is hilarious!" said Susie, watching them for a minute or two. "They did this when you were a camper, too? How did it start?"

"I don't know. I don't think it's to speed up the line, necessarily…or annoy the meal-ticket taker. It's just something to do to pass the time."

We hiked back to our food line, which had moved along, with Clare already inside. At the entrance door I spotted Dude, the operetta and play director; he was chatting with Rita, the young, statuesque blonde from Minnesota who was the staff meal-ticket taker. The two of them were a hoot—Rita always quick enough to be able to carry on a running dialogue with Dude, the two entertaining us with their innocent repartee during our waits in the staff food line.

Dude loved returning to camp each summer, and he was a natural charmer and a magnet for the staff females. In his late 30s, with clean Gene Kelly looks, he'd mastered the cool, deadpan college professor/stage director role, and flirtations simply came to him—in droves. We all needed the playful release of teasing and flirting; it was a tangible reassurance that this wasn't a colony of locked-down, repressed art drones. Not entirely, anyway.

Susie and I got our food and found a table near the lakeside windows.

"It's funny, Susie, I still feel a little in awe of Dude," I began. "Remembering his operetta productions from my camper summers—it's been so interesting getting to know him now that I'm on staff."

"Dude's a wonderful man. You know, he is amazing at San Diego State during the winter, teaching, directing shows," said Susie, softening her voice a little, "but it seems like camp is even more fun for him."

Of course, Dude was the reason Susie and so many of the others were there. It didn't take much persuasion for the students at the university to believe that he was on to something in trundling off to northern Michigan every summer.

"Who'd have thought anyone dressed in a baggy old camp uniform could have that much charisma and get everyone so riled up to work their asses off every summer, huh?" I said.

"Fershure!" Susie answered, a Californian right on cue.

HOW COULD I GET THIS FAR and not say something about the lost-in-time uniforms? The best way to visualize them might be by looking at a still of a Jeanette MacDonald–Nelson Eddy movie set at a forest campground, just as the talkies were emerging.

Everyone wore light blue short-sleeve shirts. Boys and men were outfitted in dark blue corduroys. And the girls and staff women wore...dark blue corduroy knickers. Knickerbocker Kid ragtime-era knickers, not pedal pushers — old-fashioned boy-knickers, complete with five snaps at each hip. These were completed by color-coded knee socks that indicated Junior, Intermediate, high school, or university/ staff status. Two sets of uniforms for each camp member.

The old wives' tale/folk legend explanation for knickers was that they were more appropriate, modest practice clothes for girl cellists. Parents and tourists found the camp "costume" peculiar, and one can only imagine what campers arriving from the United Kingdom thought when they read that girls were allowed to wear only knickers around camp as their standard uniform.

Camp preferred that, on Sundays, we wear white shirts brought from home, and if we needed wraps, they were supposed to be red sweaters. Very USA, very Joseph Maddy. Photos of campers used for brochures were therefore taken on Sundays, so we looked both patriotic and quaintly rustic (the knickers), like wax museum figures at an American Revolution musical theme park. Maddy, being a smart promoter, made certain to photograph campers, especially close-ups of small groups, on a regular basis.

I loved those old brochures from the 1960s

and wish I had saved more of them—they'd managed to lure me to camp in the first place, after all. The brochure photos were always models of staged improbability: six dreamy-eyed female harpists sinking into the sand by Lake Wahbekanetta, or four male bassoonists lined up near a few pine trees, the group completed by the unlikely appearance of a female dancer, en pointe in a perky red tutu, balanced atop a craggy stone wall—everyone's eyes glazed over with the sound of *music, music, music!*

Many of the photos were leaden and ordinary, but the captions were classic:

> *Exposure to music "takes" at Interlochen.*
>
> *A trio is formed with students from Austria, Japan, and Germany.*
>
> *High School Orchestra performs forty-four symphonic works in fifty-seven days.*
>
> *Junior boys excel in "he-man" sports.*
>
> *Modern dance develops physical fitness.*

By the '70s, camp owned more than ten thousand pairs of corduroys, and the inventory included very old ones mixed in with the new. The oldest trousers, while full-pleated and hot on summer days, were deep-pile, velvety-soft, wide-wale corduroy—the kind of fabric that has long since vanished from production. The shirts ranged from million-times-washed cotton to thin, filmy rayon-cotton, all with limp, flattened collars to complete the prescribed vintage arts-dork look. Some of the guys got smart and brought a set of nicely fitted modern equivalents from home. And that got noticed right away. It wasn't quite Camp Frowns, more like "Check *him* out!"

The uniforms were a source of endless discussion every summer and were an inextricable part of the identity and culture of Interlochen. I'd never worn a uniform before, and like everyone else, I came to be surprised at the freedom it imparted. Our natural tendency was to focus more on people's facial communication and personalities because we were all wearing the same absurd, almost whimsical, time-warp getup.

Years later, camp rearticulated its commitment to the uniforms; the list crackles with its own logic:

The most important aspect of wearing the uniform is neatness. From the beginning, the Interlochen uniform has meant:

> *A spirit of unity*
> *A simplified day*
> *A means of identification*
> *A blurring of class distinctions*

A simplified day—who could argue with that one?

THEATRE ARTS DEPARTMENT MEETINGS were rare—refreshingly so, compared with the dull weekly meetings I would be faced with during a brief corporate stint later in life. We knew our jobs and had plenty to do. But by now it was time for a little show of our own: the staff musical.

Robert Burroughs had been the jovial, white-haired, Santa Claus–like head of theatre arts for many years, and he loved every aspect of the theatre, from acting to design. He wore thick glasses and had an air that was comforting and paternal, if a little bumbling at times. One sunny morning he called us together on the back steps of Grunow Theatre for announcements.

"I have fabulous news.... We have cast our staff musical, *You're a Good Man, Charlie Brown*!" There was a little round of applause and cheers. "And I think we're going to make very good use of our highly talented faculty and staff. Dude is to be our Charlie Brown, Diane will play Lucy, Brent as Linus, Jay as Schroeder...with Brian as Snoopy, and our very own Sue Sanders...."

"SAUNDERS," piped up Susie with her belting, trained Dramatic Arts voice.

"Ah,   ss-suh-Saunders...as   Peppermint   Patty," Burroughs added. "Congratulations, everyone. Rehearsals start tonight, and the show goes on during the seventh week."

Later that morning I ran into Susie outside the scene shop, and the two of us ducked out of earshot of the crew.

"Susie, that was a *bit* weird—Burroughs messing up both your first and last names, calling you SUE SANDERS."

"Yeah...he was the one who hired me, right? So...Thom," Susie replied, pausing dramatically, "now I ask you...would you please tell me...if Peppermint Patty was ever even in the *Charlie Brown* musical?"

"Bogus. Why weren't you cast as Lucy? Everyone was pretty surprised. They were expecting you to get it. I have nothing against Diane...well, maybe I do; she's four times the age of Lucy and hardly what I'd call a show-sparkling ingénue type like you!"

"Thom, what can you do? It's seniority politics, sweetie. That's the way auditions go."

"It just doesn't make any sense...," I trailed off.

I felt badly for her. There was a little wordless silence between us, with moonfaced grins back and forth. "On the other hand," I offered finally, leering at her, "you get to rehearse every day with Brian-cutie."

Pause. Laughter, and then "TRUE," beamed Miss Susie, grinning radiantly like that other redheaded star of musicals, Gwen Verdon.

Brian was one of the High School Drama directors, an import from Oberlin College and a favorite of everyone that summer. His wife and two kids were just along for the ride, having a vacation—unlike the other families there, where both husband and wife were working and the kids were enrolled at camp.

If I was Susie's gay faux-brother (being another redhead), Brian was her make-believe boyfriend. He was simply a fantastically good flirt, though in reality he was a model, faithful, and high-spirited mensch of a husband/father. He and Susie were forever breaking into song, lifting lines from plays or rephrasing the most arch of camp announcements and delivering them with intentionally bad

Shakespearean accents. I might have been jealous, but their antics allowed me some rest periods in which I could just watch Susie and Brian be "on" while I sat back, a delighted audience of one.

Cabin Fevers

SOONER OR LATER during that staff summer, when there was free time and I thought I could brave it, I knew I would end up wandering over to my old high school cabin. When that time came, I left the main campus for the half-mile hike to the boys' divisions. The walk included crossing a two-lane highway and passing a foreboding state park that was more than a little David Lynch–spooky, followed by the university men's cabins, the campus classical-music radio station, and finally the All-State Boys' camp.

All-State was a two-week version of the camp experience, just for Michigan kids—which, in those days, connected Interlochen with the University of Michigan. It was a trial sampler, a kind of abbreviated Arts Lite. These kids were herded away from everything and everyone else, they dressed in non-corduroy uniforms (how Raggedy Andy, we thought), and none of the full-summer campers took too kindly to them. The path that led from the main campus to the High School Boys division went right alongside the All-State cabins, and I recall that as campers we often did a dour football-cheer singsong, loud and clear enough for their benefit:

ALLEGRO MERCATO

The All-State program was important as camp's Michigan home-state connection, but we didn't see it that way. Years later, I learned that All-Staters had their own song about the full eight-week campers; unfortunately, I never found out the words, but I am sure they captured us snotty kids very well.

I arrived at the boys' division at last and walked inside my old cabin, HSB-11. It was dark and claustrophobic inside, and even more weathered than I expected. I looked up and saw the thin plywood plank with the names of all the boys in our cabin, which I had been maneuvered into scrawling neatly with a Magic Marker during our last few days together. Now the few boys who happened to be in the cabin when I poked my head in looked alarmed—as if a surprise mattress search was about to come down. I made my best attempt at a benevolent Dad-like smile in order to becalm them.

After I adjusted a little to the whole weirdness of visiting boys' camp, a wave of memories came to me. I had gotten my friend Barry to attend camp with me, and later on talked two more pals, Duncan and Jonathan, into coming along. The other three took to the experience very much as I did. We didn't hang on to each other too much; there were a lot of funny new people to make friends with. And three of us four ended up making our lives and careers in theatre, dance, or design.

My first summer as a camper included some tense moments. I loved classes and hanging out at the theatre, but cabin life was something quite different.

My counselor, Sheldon, was a nice Jewish boy—from Canada. High School Boys Cabin 11 housed sixteen boys, ranging from Iowa and Oklahoma farm boys to a couple of smart-asses from Scarsdale and upstate New York who complained bitterly about the lack of bagels, decent or otherwise.

The New York pair and I butted heads early on, even though I too was from the East Coast. We would have heated arguments over differences of opinion on music, theatre, and art. Boys that age usually argue over who is the best baseball player, or even world politics, but at camp disagreements boiled up over things like whether Bach was the only genius composer ("the rest were just

romantic garbage") or if musical comedy could be considered *real theatre* at all.

Andy and Eddie were imperious about their artistic convictions, and our fighting matches usually escalated to the point of being vicious, personal, and quite nasty. I was confounded, miserable. No one could have warned me that I'd need debate-team skills at camp, or that I'd have to justify a love of Prokofiev and Kurt Weill just to avoid being an outcast. But I suppose I did learn a little about the way strong personality clashes can upset the apple cart.

Unlike at most camps, however, we didn't spend the majority of our time with our cabin mates. We really saw each other only for mandatory sports a few afternoons a week and at bedtime; our closest friendships were formed from our all-day classes and rehearsals and from evening performances.

When we were all together, cabin life was a sort of a parody of Boy Scout camp. Even though everyone there was busting to be a musician, actor, artist, or dancer, the boys' camp director insisted on interjecting all sorts of dumb rituals

into our days. The rituals were aimed at maintaining the program's image of wholesome outdoor life, a holdover from the 1920s and '30s, making sure camp was still camplike.

So we rose at 6:30 to a crisp, peppery, live reveille, and promptly appeared on the tennis courts in our PJs for a set of calisthenics and the day's announcements and admonishments. If my memory serves me, no one ever actually played tennis, so the courts seemed a masquerade for this other, truer function.

The breaking point, even for the marginally athletic boys, was Cabin Competition—known in camp lingo as Forced Fun. This consisted of several afternoons a week of competitive softball, soccer, volleyball, and the like. All these teenage *artiste*-boys had come to camp thinking they'd died and gone to heaven where there were no sports, and here they were once again in all their familiar terror.

The thing is, it was never a case of kids being shipped off to a camp arbitrarily selected by chilly parents; most of us had begged our parents to let us go to Interlochen so we could practice, compete, and exhaust ourselves in preparing for The Arts. Kids came home from their summer and spoke rhapsodically about it to their friends, who then often joined them the following summer. Camp probably just wanted us to write home to our folks that we were enjoying a "balanced summer." The one redemptive offering was sailing lessons, a noncompetitive, nearly solo, and pleasantly idyllic way to appreciate Lake Wahbekaness, which bordered the boys' side of the campus.

When Van Cliburn made his annual visit to Interlochen to perform, there was always a lot of chattering and whispering; the rumors flew around, especially in boys' camp, that he was gay. A six-foot-four Texan, Cliburn always

traveled with his mother and first piano teacher, Rildia Bee
Cliburn. He was still sizzling hot in America's eyes, from his
win at the Moscow 1958 Tchaikovsky International Piano
Competition, and his return to campus year after year added
a lot of luster to Interlochen. For certain, you had to give
him credit for wearing the same doggy uniform as everyone
else, including the official name badge, during his several-
day visits. He continued these appearances for eighteen
years running.

One morning midway through the summer, the division
director planned for us to have a longer-than-usual High
School Boys' meeting at sunrise. There were lots of
announcements and procedures to go over, so things were
set up so that we could have breakfast seated in our pajamas
on the tennis courts. Breakfast amounted to juice, apples,
and cartons of milk, along with miniature Kellogg's cereal
boxes that were perforated so they could be converted into
their own temporary breakfast bowls.

I was with my cabin mates, all of us crowded onto the
courts, sitting cross-legged on the asphalt in close proximity
to boys from other cabins. This was an ideal opportunity
for many of us to snicker quietly along with our alternate
voice-track of comments on the mucky-muck morning
announcements, as long as we spoke quietly enough to
escape our counselor's hearing. It was also a chance to find
out what neighboring cabins were thinking and saying.

First up was the lecture on the importance
and nonnegotiable business of participating in "Cabin
Comp" sports.

"Now listen up, men, we need to talk about something—something I know you all cherish quite a bit, Cabin Competition. I've heard all the excuses, but you've got to participate, unless you're sick or injured. And that would be only if you are admitted to the infirmary. Which I haven't heard any cases of."

"Oh, give up with it," whispered Michael, a boy from my cabin.

"I'd do anything to get out of it for the rest of the summer," I added.

"You know, David Lee got out of it, *permanently....*" Michael said.

"No way," I snapped, trying to keep my voice under the radar. "How did he manage that?"

"Well, he's only like the best high school boy pianist at camp. Turns out his hands are insured, so he's not supposed to mess around with sports at all, not even *volleyball*!" Michael explained. He stared at me, then added, "I'm serious. You think I'm joking?"

"Shh-oot!" I replied, shaking my head. "I admit, talk about brilliant...."

Several boys around us were listening in by this time, all shaking their heads, whistling, and muttering agreement over the unfairness of this clever loophole.

Counselors began glaring at us and jerking their heads in stiff upward nods, so we all acted as if nothing was going on, pretending to listen to the division leader rambling on. Out of the corner of my eye I noticed that Roger, a piano student from the next cabin, was sliding over to talk to some of my cabin mates.

"Hey. Guess what *I did* yesterday . . . ?" said Roger, in a loud stage whisper. He was a blond Scandinavian kid with large, darting eyes who was pretty sure of himself, enough so to start up a dialogue with guys from another cabin. No one answered him, but he continued anyway.

"I snuck into Van Cliburn's cabin," Roger said, grinning. He put on a bored, blasé look that I'd seen him assume before.

"No way," said Michael, my cabin mate. "He has bodyguards the whole time he's visiting. They wouldn't let anybody do that."

"Yeah. *College student* bodyguards," Roger said, tossing his head back and grinning wider than before. "Actually, it was pretty easy."

"Why . . . why did you do it?" I asked, genuinely puzzled.

"Just wanted to meet him," Roger answered.

By now, several others were listening too. They seemed enraptured with what Roger had said, and no one could think of what to ask or say next. So Roger rolled on, revealing a few more details, telling us how he jimmied a window open at the back of the cabin where pine trees obscured visibility. He said his secret in pulling it off was his "European nonchalance" and being careful not to act like "some dumb autograph seeker" once he got an audience with our visiting god of the keyboard.

Then, just as suddenly, Roger slid himself back to his cabin group, leaving us to roll our eyes or screw up our faces.

Delucci, the division leader, droned on. The morning was chilly and the meeting was as annoying as usual. I could almost predict his next topic.

"Every summer, around this time, guys, I get word from the laundry hut. Uh-huh," he whined. "They tell me they get plenty of laundry dropped off from High School Girls, but they'd really like to see your faces in there a little more often. C'mon, guys, don't make your counselors sniff your uniforms—keep 'em clean!"

Some of the boys from my cabin reclined onto the asphalt, pretending that they were falling back to sleep, so as to force an end to the torture.

"Do you think Roger's for real?" I mumbled to Michael.

"I dunno," said Michael. "Do *you*?" He looked a little freaked out.

"Eh. Maybe. He seems like someone who would make up anything. Could be, I don't know," I said, already starting to lose interest.

"But," Michael paused, "is there more...to his story? I mean, if it's true? He's from Sweden or something, right?"

"Finland, I think," I offered, giving Michael a pointed stare to let him know we weren't going to go on about it.

Whether Roger's story was true or not, we never learned any more about it. I thought of it again years later. What seemed more to the point was that it was a perfect demonstration of the ego of a young artist, and just how truly competitive they can be. Roger was out to impress us with his ambitious plan to get friendly with a concert star and be one step closer to a career of his own as a keyboard great. And, more importantly, get others to sign on to his story's spin and his ability to grab attention. If Roger didn't end up realizing his plans to be a concert pianist, he'd have made a great press agent for Pavarotti or for a scandal-plagued soprano who is forever dodging reporters and bad press.

A typical camper day ended with groups of boys taking the long, dark, shadowy walk back to our cabins after an evening's performances. There would be the final rallying sounds of us banging about, fighting over the four faucets where we brushed our teeth with water tasting of iron, and then the turning-out of bare 40-watt bulbs, one by one. Our counselor would say something dumb like "Well, gents...I want you to take a final pee now and hit the sack...or I'm giving you a rubber band for the night." And finally, after that long, exhausting, intense, and event-filled day, there was *Taps*, with the most beautiful legato trumpet playing one could possibly imagine.

One night our counselor, Sheldon, made the mistake of telling us that he would need to step out for a few hours just as we were settling down to hit the hay. He was on duty a few cabins away, doing his rotational at division headquarters. Shel would have been wiser to say nothing, wait for the first waves of snoring to start, and then slip away. Instead, he warned us that he'd keep checking in and that our cabin was within earshot of where he was to be on duty. Of course, it was an irresistible (if last-minute) dare to not be on our best behavior. Winning "Honor Cabin" wasn't exactly on anyone's mind.

I figured that as soon as Sheldon left there would be plenty of idiotic carryings-on, faked flatulence fests, and cracks about our counselor's love life, and that it would mean only that I'd get less sleep. Maybe I should even count the seconds before it started, I thought.

In fact, nothing at all happened, at least for ten or fifteen minutes. Then I heard a high-pitched tune starting to be played, softly at first but clearly coming from within our cabin. At first it sounded like a kazoo, until I realized that it was someone playing a tune into just the mouthpiece of a trumpet. It was Jerome, a goofy but ordinarily shy cabin mate.

The tune Jerome was eking out was the Interlochen Theme, which everyone grasped immediately, laughing as he continued with his squawky solo rendition. The theme was such an ever-present mantra at camp that whether you loved it or hated it, you knew it by heart. A few more bars, and everyone began humming along. Some of the boys even hummed the B-section arching harmonics of the French horns, since they were horn players and knew that orchestra part.

We all hummed along louder and louder until the piece was complete, by which time our cabin was generating quite a bit of cartoonlike orchestral sound. The neighboring cabins apparently heard us quite distinctly, because they all laughed, whistled and hollered, and finally applauded. Then—completely true to camp tradition—the other cabins, led by our own, uttered the requisite "Shhhh...!" that always followed the playing of the theme at any real camp performance, in order to prevent the tourists from polluting its sanctity with their applause.

My cabin mates howled and snickered their approval a minute or two longer, and someone whispered, "Good one, Jerome!" Then half a dozen boys promptly began faking exaggerated snores just as the cabin screen door squeaked open and flapped shut, and our counselor rushed in to find a quiet, peaceful model cabin of sixteen boys in slumber.

ONE AFTERNOON, SHELDON came into the cabin and announced, "Okay, listen up, guys.... I've got some really good news."

"Camp is discontinuing any form of sports and no longer putting saltpeter in our food?" snorted Eddie, a violist and one-half of the New York pair—the half with the most pronounced accent.

"Get serious, Eddie. No, I've arranged for us to have a cabin date with a high school girls' cabin next week."

The reaction was mixed—simultaneous whoops along with glum eye rolls and low groans. A cabin date? Can two drugstores date? What about post offices? It was a clumsy move to socialize a bunch of boys, most of whom either weren't ready for dating or were on their poky little path to coming out. But there was no getting out of it; we had to keep our date with High School Girls Cabin 8, attendance required.

The date was somewhere between a total snooze and an utter disaster. The dining hall had packed up a cold picnic version of the same crummy food. We went to the edge of the boys' lake at sunset and sat on jagged rocks. The girls assertively asked us boys questions that elicited only little grunts and nervous laughter in response. It became clear to us that the whole thing was an excuse for Shel to meet the blond female counselor of HSG-8 under charmed circumstances, where he might woo her by demonstrating his easy, natural rapport with a motley bunch of high school boy art nerds.

The few boys who had the time and the desire to date made use of two quaint camp traditions: "shake gate" and "date gate." These were two gates at the outer edges of girls' camp, which had both male and female counselor-referees on hand to monitor the high schoolers' heat. The "shake gate" was the ending place for a casual date that closed with a handshake instead of a kiss, and the "date gate" was the place for one that ended in a smooch, which of course had a strict time limit on it. I never found out if the two gates were adjacent or not.

MY SECOND SUMMER AS A CAMPER was much more fun; miraculously, I was no longer the center of derisive attacks, just an ordinary member of a reasonably harmonious cabin. I passed over theatre, majoring in radio instead. With minors in music composition (studying old rules of harmony— grueling, but my little piano trio got performed), piano tuning (hopelessly difficult, but the tools we got were very cool), and piano lessons (Debussy and Ravel that summer; my teacher from Texas insisted that my hands were nearly the size of Cliburn's—who with one hand could reach a fourteenth and glissando with it; I had hope).

Radio was a blast. Interlochen's FM public radio station manager, Richard Goerz, was articulate and no-nonsense, yet not without dry humor—and he let us take on everything that was happening at the station. The group of five boys and two girls took control of the recording booths, ripped yellow printouts of hot news and weather off the UPI teletype, and ran around campus with tape recorders doing interviews with faculty and visitors. We thought up the angles for our little spots, edited magnetic recording tape on splicing blocks, and within days heard our short programs on the air over WIAA.

The two girls in the class were live wires, a breath of fresh air amid the mostly male group of students and station staff. And we all took a keen interest when the pair thought up an idea for a short recorded piece on an occasional camp occurrence, "slumber music." Every couple of weeks during the summer, camper musicians would volunteer to perform short chamber music pieces—a string quartet or flute duet—within the high school camps at lights-out. These short, bonus lullaby recitals were yet another way for musicians to perform, and were something we all enjoyed, within the blur of so many treasured camp memories. Many years later I was amazed to discover from an old camp brochure that there had been slumber music as early as the 1940s.

For their radio piece the girls taped a few student players, mixed the music with light sounds of crickets and birds, and overdubbed short, pre-dreamtime comments from individual campers. The piece was brilliant and sincere; we played the tape over and over again, admiring what they'd done. Even the dweeby station engineers were impressed. They stood there, arms folded, nodding their heads and adjusting their thick glasses in astonishment. I was envious that the team had come up with so charming and sound-worthy an idea and managed to carry it off so well. Years later, I wished I had a copy of the tape to play again, to see if it held up across the years.

I thought that Goerz, our radio teacher, was cultured and elegant. Maybe it was because one day he had us do trial announcer readings of a weather report, and he told me I must have listened to a lot of good announcers because when I read, "And not *quite* so cool near the foothills...," I spoke with just the right amount of nuance and subtlety. We all had a crush on him.

At the end of my summer, as always, I found returning home from camp to be a bit of a letdown. Adults at Interlochen treated us like professionals in a way we never experienced at home. We'd been working at a certain level, and had gotten used to a community and an audience who seemed to get what we were doing. At Interlochen, at least, every kid was a player.

Bats, Boards, and Doodlebug

IT WAS THE MIDPOINT of my staff camp season, and already I was feeling that I didn't want it all to end too quickly. The going was good, and most everyone had found their rhythm. Besides, the performance schedule was just starting to get to the interesting stuff.

Susie had taken on the role of the redheaded showgirl posing as a seamstress (which is exactly what she was), and in the costume shop she and Clare did a lot to relieve production-schedule pressures by keeping up what amounted to an ongoing coffee klatsch/drop-in talk show, to the amusement of the other staff. They lifted plastic cherries from the prop room for seamstresses to wear as seasonal hair adornments. Care packages arrived full of things like George H. Funk granola from southern California and garlicky three bean salad and other Jewish deli goods from Detroit.

Clare, fairy godmother that she was, had rounded up a secondhand fridge within days of arriving; she loved being able to keep treats on hand, and she knew that a well-stocked fridge would be the easiest way to keep the costume crew there and working into the evening as show deadlines loomed one after another.

I hung out in the costume shop as much as I could. Everyone did; it was home. Throughout the day, as young actors were being fitted for costumes, there was laughter and a sort of running dialogue that you might stroll into, like a sitcom character entering on cue.

On this particular day, there were some visual aids too.

"Hey, Clare...I promised I'd bring in some of my show photos from San Diego," announced Susie. She fanned out a couple of three-by-five-inch black-and-white photos, and several of the costume girls slid over to silently inspect. There was a little beat of quiet and then, "Oh my...wow...Susie, these are fabulous!"

"This one is the operetta *Patience*...and that's a play about a Cherokee princess...and this one is *Guys and Dolls,* of course," Susie explained.

"You're Adelaide...BOOWANNA!—your gazongas are barely tucked into that décolletage there. I *love* it!" gushed Clare, tapping her finger on Susie's tightly costumed breasts in the photo of her from the Hotbox nightclub scene. Two of the costume assistants grabbed the photo from Clare's hands. They were like little girls grubbing over a Barbie version of a baseball card.

Clare had to study the pictures for a few more moments.

"Who took these?" she finally asked, looking up at Susie.

"Mary!" beamed Susie.

"They're wonderful. As if we needed proof you were a starlet."

"You mean you guessed I was actually an ac-tress?" teased Susie, in a pinched Betty Boop voice.

"Susanita, honey, I knew that from your first day here. I mean, anyone who reads the instructions on a box of Rit dye as if it were Noël Coward...probably ain't a seamstress at heart!"

"C'mon, my grommet work is very nice, you have to admit," protested Miss Boop.

I was passing through the costume shop on the way to the drama office to pick up my mail when I heard, "Barbarians! I can't stand it—year after year!"

It was the department secretary, Marilyn, a cheerful woman with a mop of black curly hair, who was most likely the true backbone of the department. Marilyn dealt with our shoestring budgets and the Maddy Building folks, and listened to the department head debate aloud all morning about whether he would try to sneak down to the Fisher Theatre in Detroit to catch a pre-Broadway musical. On the other hand, she did seem to come back year after year, along with her husband, who worked in the university division, slumming at Interlochen from his winter job as a chorus member of the Metropolitan Opera.

Marilyn's yelps in the office were alarming enough that Clare followed me in to find out what was happening.

"Marilyn, what in the devil is going on? Is everything

OK?" quizzed Clare, owl-eyed.

"Oh, Lordy... I just got a call from Jay at Stage Services. He's trying to round up a crew of guys to help wipe out the bats in Kresge tonight. It is so sick.... I'll be darned if I walk across to the scene shop and recruit anyone for this nonsense!"

It was a fifth-week camp ritual that most people could have lived without. The yearly tradition was that a bunch of volunteers would pitch in to diminish the bat population prior to the operetta performances.

We'd gotten pretty used to bats swooping in on Beethoven now and then, but I guess the added lighting of the big production made the bats more of an annoyance than usual. And they could frighten the knickers (or gowns) off Mabel or Buttercup during a performance.

So every year, an ad hoc band of young staff men gathered late at night and secured "bat boards" (were they special boards, bloodied, dried off, and stored from year to year? I didn't care to know) and spent the witching hour creating carnage on Kresge's stage, beneath one-foot-tall lettering across the back wall that read "Dedicated to the Promotion of World Friendship Through the Universal Language of the Arts."

I'm sure the bat boys thought they were saving the day for everyone, but it all seemed more like a brief show of testosterone from a stagehand's worldview of operetta.

Progress marched along in my own world of props and stagecraft. Between struggling with creating a Biedermeier coffin, constructing a handheld replica of the Statue of

Liberty torch, and tracking down percolator coffee pots and an ear trumpet, I rode out to the scenic storage warehouse on a goofy small tractor called the Doodlebug, which pulled a series of flatbed cars toting scenery and furniture. Another wartime surplus item in full usage, Miss D's engine front was painted with kewpie-doll eyes and enormous eyelashes; it was an amusement park ride exclusively for camp's theatre staff, who were often seen tearing across campus at top speed, scenery flats flapping in the wind for dear life.

As each production entered final rehearsals, I would finish preparing props and move into setting up backstage and helping students learn the ropes in order to run the shows on their own. Getting backstage set up always involved creating a secret funhouse of design and ingenuity. Each play required a customized maze of scenic components, lighting pipes, teaser and tormenter masking drapes, prop tables, and a few jerry-rigged solutions to help with a production's stagecraft demands.

A flight of stairs onstage would lead to a doorway to nowhere—or, rather, to a raised platform and a set of "escape stairs" that enabled actors to return to stage level. Pipes and obstructions often needed to have foam-rubber pads affixed to them to prevent injuries in the dark. Quirky alert signs, created by the camper crew, would be affixed to scenery and lights backstage. "DO NOT SIT HERE unless you are MARIAN THE LIBRARIAN" read a boldly markered sign on the back, upstage side of a porch swing. The scorching light-dimmer banks sported one reading "WARNING, SHE'S A HOT ONE, mind your cords!"

For the upcoming play, two girls and a boy would take on the roles of stage manager, prop master, and runner/ assistant; Bob worked with two more kids to run the lights. Some of the drama majors might have preferred to be in the play rather than to help run backstage, but it was always better to be involved in a show and feel part of a production. Final dress rehearsal was a day away, so this was the moment for me to familiarize the small crew with the setup. They were eager to learn all the tricks; it was time for the tour.

"You need to know every inch of backstage," I explained to them. "It's very tight once everything is in place for performance, and it'll be dark. And there is that one extra twist back here to make things just a little bit tougher."

"The actors!" blurted the taller girl.

"You got it," I smiled. "But they'll end up needing your help more than they realize."

"I hope so," said the younger boy, making a face. "Right now during rehearsals, we're pretty much ignored."

I couldn't help relating to his remark, laughing a little before continuing with my spiel.

"Your main necessities are the marked script notebook, the cue sheets, a blue-gel flashlight, and two kinds of tape," I went on.

"Why two kinds?" asked one of the girls.

"Gaffer's tape is best for light pipes, or anything involving weight that needs strength. And the silver surface of it shows up better in the dark, to mark things that actors might run into."

They all bobbed their heads in agreement, standing

by for more.

"And the black tape is for covering stuff that shouldn't show, things that are in the wings within the stage sight lines. Really, though, you can use this tape for just about anything, especially emergencies."

The younger girl and the boy looked a little worried. The girl asked, "What kind of emergencies? You mean like a broken chair leg or something?"

"Mmm, yeah, well, maybe. You could also make something out of it, like if a prop went missing at the very last second," I said. "My job is to get all the props made and assembled for the plays, and you guys take charge of them in performance. You have to keep a sharp eye on everything. Props have an annoying tendency to walk off, if you know what I mean," I continued. They smiled and nodded. I could see they were beginning to get into the spirit of their jobs.

"Some of the props we'll have duplicates for, but that'll be our little secret. If anything is missing, everyone blames the stage manager or the prop master, even if it is one of the actors who misplaces a prop during a performance. You've got to be super-prepared," I explained.

"But you said you might need the tape in case you had to…'make something' last-minute," the boy reminded me.

"Right. Okay, so let's imagine that, just a few minutes before an actor is to go on, the pistol is suddenly missing from this organized, labeled prop table. You could swear it was *right there* a minute ago. What are you going to do?" I asked them. "The show must go on, right?"

There was no response. The younger two kids looked to

the older girl, the stage manager.

"The answer is, you're going to make a gun prop as fast as you can using black tape and whatever else you can find backstage. So...let's try it," I said.

I handed each of them a roll of black tape and a couple of pencils, and checked my watch pointedly, saying, "Okay, I'm giving you four minutes. Do the best you can to make a prop pistol out of just the tape and pencils."

"Oh, no!" said the younger girl, her face a disaster.

All three looked panicked but scrambled for the prop table to go to work.

I enjoyed watching them take on my challenge. Right away, two of them snapped the pencils sharply in half. Each would look up and take note of what the others were doing, then return to fiddling and forming a gun shape before there was too much time to think about what they were trying to do.

The boy was a natural. He wrapped tape around and around his skeletal gun form until it was bloated and huge. Then he pushed and sculpted the mass like modeling clay until it was just the way he wanted, punching holes at the end to form space for the trigger.

"Time's up!" I said. "Let's see what you've got."

One of the creations looked like a Sputnik, another like an amorphous giant licorice shape. The third was nothing short of amazing.

"Mark, you did a great job," I said. "You threw yourself into this. I'm impressed!"

Mark grinned, looking dumbfounded, and the two

girls took turns handling the magical prop that had been produced at lightning speed. After a moment or two, a critic emerged.

"But even Mark's doesn't look as good as the prop gun," the older girl said timidly.

"No, but it will work just fine. The actor whose gun is missing is going to be happy to have any kind of prop at all in his hand, rather than having to make up new lines onstage or reblock his stage business at the last minute," I explained. "In the dramatic moment, the context, this gun will be fine onstage. The audience will accept it. They are expecting it to be there. And the actor will probably keep the pistol in his upstage hand, so it's not in view the whole time."

They nodded, weighing what I'd said.

We walked around backstage as I tried to explain the need to appear cool and confident while running the show, and about learning to invent and use wordless communication across the stage from stage left to stage right, since not everyone would wear headsets. They were especially interested in the business of creating and preparing stage food and fake beer, several sets of which were stored in the costume shop below. The beer had to look foamy enough and not like a soft drink; the sandwiches weren't to be too dry—or too taste-tempting (either to the actor they were intended for or to anyone backstage considering a midshow snack).

The three of them sat on the apron of the stage so I could talk them through responsibilities and have time to work in their other questions. Their legs dangled over the edge of the stage; they were careful not to swing their feet back. By that time, they knew it would scuff up the black of the stage risers. I sat in a seat in the front row, facing them.

"So Bob will be in the light booth with a student crew member running the follow spot," I said.

"Are you...will you be backstage with us, too?" asked the younger girl.

"I'll be around. But you guys are running the show!" I answered. "I know you guys will handle everything fine, but you have to expect that little things are going to happen."

I could see that the three were getting anxious all over again. The camper stage manager spoke.

"We don't have to go onstage if...like one of the actors faints or something, do we?" she asked.

"Ha, that's a good question. It's always been theatre tradition that the stage manager goes on for an actor who for any reason can't make it onstage at the very last minute. In a situation like that, the stage manager would need to stand onstage and read from a script, making no pretense at acting,

just filling in the dialogue. But you're not going to have to worry about that," I said.

"How do you *know* that?" asked the boy.

"Haven't you ever wondered why there are no understudies in High School Drama for any of the plays?" I quizzed them.

All three looked blank, then slowly nodded their heads.

"You know how drama majors are here. They've been dreaming of this all winter long. They'd sooner kill themselves than miss a performance!"

We all laughed. They were looking bright and confident again. Then Bob and one of the lighting assistants emerged from the booth at the back of the theatre.

"Hey, guys. How's it all look?" I yelled back to them. "Making popcorn yet?"

"Yeah, maybe at dress/tech tonight," answered the female crew member who was assisting. "You're right, the follow spot just gets so hot!"

She was skinny and had large black oven mitts on her hands. One of the student crew sitting with me started giggling.

"She looks," Lisa said, under her breath, "... like *Minnie Mouse!*"

All four of us started to laugh as quietly as we could. What Lisa had said was true enough, what with the follow-spot operator's wiry frame, knickers, and oversized dark mitten-hands.

"Well, that's pretty much it. Be alert, listen, and know the dialogue so that you're ready to execute your cues. And remember that the goal is for things to go smoothly backstage and *onstage*, too."

"Onstage, too?" asked the younger girl.

"It might not seem like it, but you and the actors are performing together. It's one dance you're all doing," I said. "Have you ever seen one of those big Chinese snakes—maybe in the Thanksgiving parade on TV—with ten or twelve people all holding up the snake on poles above their heads? Everyone is needed to create the illusion; they're all gliding forward, coordinating, and looking up so they can smooth out little chain-reaction movements and get the serpent to slither, floating in the air above. That's what it's like running the show, timing your light and sound cues, the blackouts, even the final curtain, all happening on just the right beat."

"Huh," said one of them. I detected a few faint signs of blue flashlights glimmering in their eyes.

Five performances later, the camper stage crew had become a tight-knit little team, reveling in the details and precision of their stagecraft. They'd have been happy to have the play run all summer long. As part of "crew pride," the kids wore their headsets throughout the day, even to lunch, and they'd inserted blue lighting gels into the name slots of their three-inch-round camp identity badges, covering the rest of the badges with black tape. Two of the kids ended up tossing a coin after the final performance to see who would get to keep the faked tape stage pistol.

"We did slip the taped gun into the final performance," the camper stage manager told me later. "Nobody noticed, not even the director."

"I kept hoping some uppity parent would come back and tell us kids we shouldn't be using real guns onstage,"

Mark added, "...'cause I would love to have handed them this one and have 'em see that it's just a wad of tape!"

BOB AND I FORMED AN EASY FRIENDSHIP, working together every day at the theatre and running performances. During the early weeks of camp I'd thought him a decent guy, if taciturn—keeping to himself the way a lighting/tech guy might. As it turned out, the Susie effect brought out another, unexpected side of Bob.

He and I were stashed in the same staff cabin quarters, which had rough-hewn shared-cubicle rooms for eight. One Sunday, I was lying in my bunk dozing in the afternoon when I heard little cat scratches on my window screen, followed by a high-pitched voice saying softly, "T-T-Thommeee...Thommykins?," the T's being front-loaded in the style of Double Dutch jump-rope girls.

Slowly awakening, I pulled up the rough muslin drape and saw Susie attempting to jump into her wooden clogs with a running leap from ten or fifteen feet away. Immediately, without warning, she and Bob fired up in musical-comedy mode, striking *Show Boat* poses and launching into full-throated Al Jolson–style song. The beauty of being part of the theatre staff was that it was more fun to live up to the cliché people had of you than to bother trying to fit in. We had uniforms for that.

Bob and Susie were successful, as usual, in aborting my quiet time and getting me out to cavort with them, all three of us acting like overgrown, out-of-control Junior campers.

As it was our only real full day off, we decided on impulse to dash into town and catch a revival of Ken Russell's *The Boy Friend,* which was showing in a tiny movie theater. The movie's campy lunacy hit the right note for the mood of the day, and we roared back to camp in the car singing "A Room in Bloomsbury" at the top of our lungs, before Bob decided to head back to the theatre to take advantage of the empty stage and finish hanging lights for the upcoming show.

Susie and I tagged along, knowing that Bob would be grateful for a real body or two moving about the stage to ensure evenness and focus of the lights. I'd figured by this point that our antics had come to an end, at least for that day. But there *was* already a piano onstage for the rehearsals of *The Music Man.* I had eyed it, and I knew Susie had, too.

Once the planes of light were starting to cooperate, I sat down at the piano and played a version of what is called (at the close of nearly every musical-comedy score) "Music for Bows." Susie dashed on from the wings and bowed grandly and theatrically in as hammy, Bernadette Peters–like a manner as possible. She was, after all, the actor-hopeful among us. Bob rallied once more, joining in the bows, in Robert Preston mode. Then I followed, as Tommy Tune, of course. We were extremely precise and perfectly in sync, and we just howled and did it over and over again until Bob finally kicked us out to finish his work.

A Bounty of Barns and Fairies

AUDIENCES ALWAYS SEEMED to either love or hate Gilbert and Sullivan. But it was practically a moot point at Interlochen, because a certain amount of production values, not to mention cast members, went into the annual high school light opera offering. Even by 1929, camp's second season, there was a staged *Pirates of Penzance*, thus beginning an annual G&S tradition.

I was beginning to tire of the big three (*Pinafore, Pirates, Mikado*), so it was a relief to learn that this year the operetta workshop would be putting on *Iolanthe*. Originally written as a parody of the British Parliament, *Iolanthe* contains references that are lost to us now, but it is the mother of all fairy romps in opera, light or otherwise. As if operetta isn't gay enough, this particular one is more like the gay standard.

My first brush with *Iolanthe* had been at camp in '65, when it was performed in a truncated version by the Intermediate operetta workshop. The one thing I remembered from that production was that at the moment all of Parliament is transformed into fairies in order to fly off to fairyland, ingeniously camouflaged wings were unsnapped to unfold from the backs of all the boys' jackets. One of those boys—a thirteen-year-old lead actor—was Tom Hulce, who years later would be nominated for an Oscar for portraying Mozart in the film *Amadeus*.

The unquestioned maestro and creative force behind all of this was Dude, who had been staging and directing these Busby Berkeley–style extravaganzas year after year. He, too, was probably happy to be doing one of the less performed, sillier operettas. During the winter he directed college drama majors in musicals, but he came into his element when faced with the challenge of bringing life into these old G&S chestnuts at Interlochen.

In staging the operettas, Dude also had a lot of bodies to work with: typically about a hundred and twenty girls and twenty or thirty boys. After you sorted out the trained voices and patter song–equipped males, what do you do with the rest of the troops?

Dude's answer was evident at the first performance, which took place on a beautiful, breeze-filled evening. I sat in the audience with our usual little gang. Even Mary, who'd seen more of these than anyone, wanted to find out what twists and turns Dude would devise each year.

In *Iolanthe* there is a moment in Act I when Strephon—who is half fairy (his fairy mother married a mortal)—needs to summon his mum to intervene in his predicament (definitely shades of Samantha in *Bewitched*). The music at this juncture, wonderfully airy and Mendelssohnian, reaches a climax, at which point the fairies are to enter en masse as quickly as possible.

Dude was always one to use the space, and Kresge's stage was nearly the width of Radio City Music Hall. Suddenly, two rows of sixty fairies each came running, cascading along the top of the low concrete walls on both of the open-air sides of the amphitheater. All were wearing panels of tutti-frutti minty colors, singing their fluty entrance in sonic, chirpy waves of pastels:

> *Tripping hither, tripping thither,*
> *Nobody knows why or whither;*
> *We must dance and we must sing*
> *Round about our fairy ring!*

The fairies were set against the sunset sky on either side of the theatre, breezes billowing all those filmy costumes, making them look like dozens of Isadora Duncans refracted and multiplied in a hall of mirrors. The antiphonal effect of so many voices singing in thirds was like lush ribbon candy. Kresge's cavernous acoustics were finally good for something other than symphonic brass passages, and Dude had maximized the effect to both hilarious and thrilling advantage. It was all surreal, better than a music video—it was live.

The performance left us with such a high that we had to go out afterward. Dude was really a day person, giving

110 percent to campers and class, so I knew he wouldn't join us. Instead, Mary, Bob, Susie, and I hauled out of Dodge hoping we could find some night eatery still open that would suit the crew. None of us wanted to go to the Hofbrau; it was just down the road from camp and a magnet for parents and tired-out counselors. Karlin Inn was an option, but somebody said it was closed that night. No matter, Mary knew the perfect spot.

We were pushing seventy on dark, unlit country roads, Mary once again at the wheel. "It's pretty near here now," she murmured. "Wow, look to the right, wild blueberries. We've got to come back here and pick some later this week."

We drove another minute and suddenly, without warning, Mary swerved violently off the road right into a field of very tall grasses, still flooring it.

"Woahhhh!" I gasped, bracing my arm against the dash.

"Mary, what the hell?!" shrieked Susie.

"Barn!" Mary barked.

Mary kept on driving another two hundred feet, weeds thrashing loudly, violently against the windshield and body of the car, the vehicle finally slowing up near a dark, dilapidated structure.

"God, Mary, you and your barnstorming," snorted Susie. "Couldn't you have just pulled off to the side of the road instead of doing a Hitchcock on us?!"

"Yeah, sorry, it's just that I love to photograph old barns, and if I see a good one, I like to take a closer look, then come back later with my camera."

"Like in the *daytime*, Mary?" pleaded Susie. "I thought we were going to eat?"

I don't remember exactly how, but Mary backed up the car, turned it around, and got us back on the road. Once we realized that she wasn't certifiable, terror gave way to laughter and relief. Minutes later we were at a pine-paneled greasy spoon with the requisite beat-up jukebox turned up full blast.

Settling into red vinyl dinette chairs, we seized the worn menus and ordered a massive pig-out of mismatched items. It was like a trap going off, our cutting out once more from the Sanctuary of Rules, and we all started talking at once.

"What—a—great—night," I began.

"Unbelievable...Dude has outdone himself," Susie added.

"He's such an ace at the big productions,"agreed Bob.

"Didn't the girl who played the fairy queen remind you of one of those porcelain Christmas trees with built-in lights—in that enormouscostume?" I said.

"But my God,

what a great big, booming low voice she had!" said Susie.

"Don't you love it? She's like sixteen or seventeen and gets up there wearing twenty pounds of costume and performs to a big, dark cavern with several thousand people watching," said Mary.

"Pure genius, a total camp," I continued.

"It would have been so easy to screw up the whole thing," added Susie, "but that's Dude for you."

"Did you catch those staff women ushers policing the aisles to make sure there was room for all the fairies to come through? Too funny," Bob exclaimed.

"Cobblers or matrons?" quizzed Susie in a sharp, urgent voice.

"WHAAT?" interrupted Mary. Susie and I burst out laughing.

"Mary, you've never heard Susie and me say that before?" I answered. "Our names for whether a staff woman is wearing knickers or a corduroy skirt uniform?"

"No!" said Mary. "I . . . I mean, that's too much!" erupting into her usual jelly pot of giggles.

"Think about it. It really makes sense," I said. "Especially the older staff women in knickers always look as if they're shuffling around like a cobbler . . . or like Geppetto!"

"And the corduroy skirts always make women look like den mothers or *somebody's* mother," Susie added.

There were snorts of laughter as we dove into the food arriving at our table—a late-night-snack array of pancakes, French fries, muffins, Cokes, and a blueberry milkshake.

"Well, here it is . . . already the end of the sixth week,"

Mary sighed, biting into a blueberry muffin that had been amply slathered with butter.

"Yeah... and Bob and I have even managed to keep our mustaches this long," I offered cheerfully.

Bob, Susie, and I laughed.

"What do you mean?" asked Mary, earnest and wide-eyed.

"Well, noises have been made to both Thom and me, but I sure as hell wasn't going to shave mine off!" said Bob, grinning from beneath his ample 1970s walrus.

"Camp Frowns? Screw camp!" I added loudly; our waitress looked up suddenly from the front of the restaurant. She'd already pegged us as folks from *that music camp.*

"Ridiculous. They're still at it with those ancient camp rules?" said Mary, in heated disbelief.

"The camp line is that 'no mustaches' is an important part of 'neatness,' blah blah blah. Jeez, maybe I signed in my contract about wearing the uniform, but I know I didn't sign anything about 'no facial hair.' It can't be legal, can it?" I mused.

"We just ignore 'em," snickered Bob. "As if they would fire their lighting and prop guys..."

"For God's sakes," Mary added. "I mean, goatees and beards are practically standard on some of those faculty and visiting conductors. It's kind of like they're saying that staff are really still campers—how insane!"

"We're ever youthful. You have to laugh. Camp is, as usual, hilariously out of touch," I said. "Let's face it—I mean, GAY doesn't exist at camp because SEX doesn't exist to begin with!"

"National Neuter Camp! Center for Asexual Studies!" piped up Susie, joining in the attack.

This was followed by a round of even louder, extended laughter. Our waitress, looking genuinely pained, checked her wristwatch against the wall clock and darted into the kitchen.

"Wait, you guys—I heard something last summer, you'll love this," said Mary excitedly. "I was talking with Peg from the Maddy Building one day, and she reminded me that there was a movie made in the '40s that was based on Interlochen!"

"You're kidding!" hissed Susie.

"Apparently camp had artistic say in the script. And the movie's story line had a romance between two campers— which Maddy vetoed—so it was cut out altogether!" said Mary.

"Oh my god. Typical!" I said.

"So you see," Mary continued, "it's the same thing year after year. It's camp tradition. They make sure of that."

"Mmm, right...but Mary—hold on, you've been coming here like... FOREVER. None of it has driven you away," I protested.

"And what about you, Thom, you're back again," said Mary, "right?"

She had me. I shot back a goofy, caught look and finally responded, "I dunno. Honestly, it's hard for me to figure out quite how or why I came back. Chalk it up to the call of the pines. I'm hooked, I guess. Pretty dumb, huh?"

Our post-party was winding down, though I probably could have sat there yakking and gorging on starch, sugar, and salty food all night. Mary somehow delivered us back to our little toy cabins, and we drifted off under piles of blankets before another week struck up, *molto allegro con fuoco*.

Drama and Music

THE MUSIC MAN WAS A HIT. Every summer the arrival of the high school musical is a much-anticipated camp event, not just for the drama folks. It's showtime without even a hint of corduroy, just like the real thing. I loved running that show, as did all of the student stage crew. Weird but true—musicals are even more fun from backstage than out front, because of the group spirit and the unseen backstage version of the choreography accompanied by all that live, sloshy, singable music.

There was a wonderful irony in camp's putting on this musical, as Joseph Maddy was a sort of Harold Hill in reverse. In the musical, Hill is a traveling-salesman swindler who goes from town to town, selling the parents on uniforms and instruments that are never delivered, banking on his bogus Think Method and parental pride to create the illusion that the town's kids could form a band and learn to play music.

Maddy also found parents and campers eager to fall under his spell, but he provided the uniforms (and many of the instruments), and he enlisted genuinely talented young players. Instead of the Think System, he developed an actual methodology of teaching music with Thaddeus P. Giddings, camp cofounder and coauthor with Maddy of the groundbreaking *Universal Teaching* book series. Where Maddy's salesmanship was needed was in finding donors to support the notion of a camp through thick and thin, and he stayed put to make it all happen.

The set designer for *The Music Man* made sure that Grunow Theatre grew arms and legs for the musical, as an old black-and-white photo shows. The town of River City, Iowa, burst well beyond the left and right edges of the proscenium, with additional playing areas added to the stage set to allow for the large cast and hyperactive choreography.

Miss Adrianne had drawn out every ounce of high school adrenaline for the dance numbers, proving herself worthy of all her manic intensity. Her dancers were convinced that she was a real former Broadway gypsy, whether that was true or not, and they followed suit, delivering piston-hot performances. I loved walking back to the theatre when rehearsals were in progress, hearing show songs and feeling the tuneful toy theatre rock on its foundation—like a television cartoon of a house, with commotion going on inside and wavy motion lines, O's and X's, emanating all around it.

A few days after the fuss and flurry of *The Music Man*, High School Drama put together an extra showcase performance, a variety show. Actors who had completed their performances for the summer were only too willing to seize another opportunity to get onstage, and this thrown-together show provided another look at the young performers in vignettes tailored to their own particular talents.

At the performance, I couldn't think of anyone I'd rather sit alongside than Susie and Brian, to watch monologues and a number of songs and ballads from musicals and operettas— some of which had likely been the well-tuned audition pieces of the campers. One of the most talented boys outdid his earlier performances with his comic timing and rendition of "I'm an Ordinary Man" from *My Fair Lady*. By coincidence, two girls had planned to perform the same ballad, so they ended up singing it together, alternating lines of the lyrics with a double tragicomic twist.

But the dance solo was the surprise of the ad hoc program. The taped music of Saint-Saëns' *The Swan* began to play, a signal that we were about to see a rendition of Pavlova's Dying Swan solo. Every camp person knew this music, evidenced by the fact that it drew a number of undisguised groans from the mostly teenage audience.

"Achh," whispered Susie to Brian and me. "Is she going to do this for real?"

"I'm not sure," I murmured.

The dancer fluttered lightly onto the stage in her tutu, the costume completed by a white feathered skullcap surrounding her ballerina assoluta white face and engraved red lips. So far, it all looked to me as though we were headed for a painful cornball solo, although the actress clearly had more than a bit of ballet training.

About a half minute into the solo, the dancer's face suddenly stretched like Lucille Ball's as she eyed a white thread hanging from the end of one of her pointe shoes. She bourréed to the side of the stage near the proscenium and did a little head jerk and eye roll in the direction of her shoe, whereupon a stagehand's arm reached out of the wings to try to remove the thread.

The dancer gently glided en pointe back to the center of the stage, the dismembered hand still holding onto the errant thread, yards of which were emerging from her shoe as she moved. Pockets of the audience were erupting in giggles and recognition that a sly parody was in progress.

The ballerina continued, trying to ignore the difficulty. Then she began doing various footwork in hopes of breaking the nasty, never-ending thread. She raised and waved her leg in a wild, very unswanlike rond de jambe/cancan. Having failed, she then tried to sever the thread with her other foot—while still trying to make her desperate footwork seem as though it *might* be part of the choreography. Meanwhile, two arms were now visible at the edge of the proscenium, madly pulling away, as yards and yards of the white thread continued to emerge from the confounded toe-shoe floss dispenser.

The four-minute solo was nearly over, and the dancer's anguished face necessarily gave in to her portrayal of the swan's dying moments. The ballerina slowly melted to a seated swan pose on the stage floor, arms fluttering, resigned to both her swan's and her toe shoe's fate.

Just as the music finished—miraculously—the end of the thread appeared at last. The swan was free now to meet her maker. The audience erupted with applause and tears of laughter, stomping their feet on the floorboards of the house with approval. The prima ballerina emerged from the wings for her bow, staying in character—gripping the proscenium with one hand and keeping her tortured dancer face, which glanced in melodramatic jerks all about the house and to a nonexistent balcony, every inch the Russian ballerina ham.

On our way out of the theatre, Susie, Brian, and I agreed that we had stumbled into the most entertaining and wicked four minutes of the summer's abundantly rich performance schedule. Wonderful moments onstage, whether performed by students or professionals, can live a long time in memory if they are vivid and perfectly presented. Some thirty years later, I emailed another camp pal—who was by then a veteran New York choreographer—and we both remembered, and regaled in having seen this Dying Swan comedy miniature. It wasn't exactly what Interlochen was famous for, but it was memorable nonetheless.

THE FOLLOWING DAY, with the variety show in the
bag and the fourth of the main productions up and running,
a couple of us had made a pact that no matter how busy we
were, we would cut out one afternoon to catch one other
performance, the Junior Drama presentation of several fairy
tales. Things were hectic that day, so we invoked the second
part of our pact, which was to not tell anyone where we were
that afternoon and arrive separately. The latter part was
tricky but not impossible, with all the footpaths weaving
each of the different camp areas together.

I was returning from the scenery warehouse, walking
through the main campus, when I noticed Mary sitting
in the sun, reading a book, in front of Beethoven—the
perfunctory cement-block faculty/staff residence she stayed
in each summer. There was a strange, beautiful, and eerie
music coming from Kresge Auditorium nearby.

"Hey!" I yelled.

"Hey!" Mary called back, looking up with her huge
smile. I darted over and joined her on the bench.

"Mary, you look so relaxed and dreamy just sitting here
in the sun. Like some photo in a brochure for a sanitarium,
with tea arriving soon."

Mary giggled. Her laugh lines always seemed an
invitation to linger awhile.

"What is that incredible music playing?" I asked her.

"Isn't it amazing?" Mary said, aglow. "It's that
visiting Indonesian gamelan orchestra rehearsing for their
performance tonight. Wonderful..."

"Wow," I said.

I realized I had never really had a quiet moment with Mary all summer long. She was always surrounded by people, laughter, and group goings-on; the strange music seemed to underscore the pleasantness of our unexpected rendezvous. For all the wildness at camp, there were also moments of real serenity.

"So, how's it going? You've been enjoying your summer?" Mary asked.

"Oh God, none of us want it to end. What about you?" I asked.

"Fan-*tas*-tic," she said. "I've been running around doing so much crazy stuff this year, I've hardly seen my other half."

"You've been having fun working and hanging out with Jon, right?" I said.

"Jon is a sweetheart," she answered.

Jon was from Berkeley, a scene painter and member of the stage crew. He and I got along fine; we were about the same age. To my tastes, he was too blond, too nice, and seemed to talk only in surfer-speak, but then again, it was 1972.

Jon had taken to Mary just as we all had; she always seemed so upbeat, curious, and all-embracing in her approach to people. If Mary liked him, in the end, that counted for something.

"Well, I've got to run. A few of us promised that we'd pop over to see the Junior Drama today. See you later, Mary.... Enjoy your reading in the sun."

"Fershure!" Mary flashed a wide grin, her eyes following me as I walked along Percy Grainger Lane toward the Junior division, the Indonesian music trailing behind me like a subtle perfume.

I passed the pine log-cabin studio of camp's longtime piano/harpsichord teacher George Luckenberg, whose funky painted "Harpsicart" van was parked nearby. When I was halfway to Junior camp, I felt an incredibly strong sense of déjà vu from my own camper summers that made me stop and stand motionless, not unlike the chipmunks at camp that would seem to freeze and turn into decorative figurines if they spied you getting near them.

There was a stretch of woods that was mostly made up of faculty music-studio cabins. Emanating from them during the day was a combination of dozens of sound snippets...classical piano, woodwinds, strings, and

horns...big juicy teases of Chopin and Brahms...all weaving among the trees with only a trace of an echo. Eerie because you couldn't detect the location of any one instrument; for me, this enchanted musical forest was always one of the ravishing, unique features of an Interlochen summer.

The Junior Drama presentation, a series of fairy tales

put on by third- through sixth-graders, was
heartfelt and disarming. The audience sat on
wooden chairs, and the tiny performers
appeared on a small curtained stage at
one end of a rustic assembly hall with tall, gabled ceilings.
Somehow I just felt grateful that the Juniors, little prodigies
or not, were allowed to play and perform in a simple, humble
setting that included all the cozy, familiar trappings of an
ordinary children's summer camp. They would advance to
those stern teachers and long hours of work soon enough.

Kids of that age, with all their excitement about being
on stage, tended toward the familiar school of overacting.
Which is what made it so interesting to be able to spot the
quieter focus and talent of the girl playing Little Red Riding
Hood, as well as the boy narrator. Even at this age, their
natural sense of poise and stage presence set them apart
and caught the eye of audiences and teachers. It was a little
marvel in itself to see these tiny seeds that might lead to a
lifetime in the theatre after their start here at camp.

IT ALWAYS SURPRISED ME how many of the faculty
gave performances at camp—something that isn't always the
case at universities. I often wondered if the administration
had dictated "perform or perish" to each new hire. And
it was inspiring to see not only recorded artists and well-
known performers but also academic teachers bring on the
bravura and subject themselves to the scrutiny of young,
often tough audiences.

During my high school summers, my piano teacher, David Appleby, presented a program of all Brazilian music—something that wasn't performed or recorded nearly so often in those days. Afterward, I felt quite differently about him as a teacher, and my piano teachers back home suddenly seemed quite provincial and conservatory-like in comparison. I couldn't imagine them on a stage mashing up Mussorgsky or slicing through Scriabin.

It was anticlimactic when the drama faculty and staff finally performed the *Charlie Brown* musical. I hadn't seen any rehearsals, so I was somewhat unprepared. The cast was up to it, but there was something a little odd about twenty- to forty-year-old adults playing seven-year-old kids—for an audience that included a fair share of seven-year-olds. The fatal mistake was putting the intimate little musical on the enormous Kresge stage, an ill-conceived notion from the get-go.

The production was too well lit and excessively miked. The performers, in their bright, primary-color costumes, looked like six leftover French fries burning up under a fast-food heat lamp. But perhaps it's good for students to see something that doesn't all come together, too. So many concerts and performances were crammed into one summer at Interlochen that the journey was clearly the reward. It would be missing the point to get precious about anything. Summer's pace really did seem a bit like another of Maddy's famous mottos, "Learn more in less time."

THE CREW BACK AT THE THEATRE was getting more and more slaphappy. Excuses for any impromptu escapade seemed to be the rule. We'd gotten to the point where we'd been working very hard and were tired of putting off some of the things we'd promised to slip in by summer's end.

On Monday, our half workday, the Grunow staff came together, taking a unified stand against the dining hall food with our own big-salad bacchanal. Everyone rooted around at roadside produce stands just outside of camp to be sure we included bodacious beefsteaks, really real lettuce greens, and scallions with the dirt still clinging to their roots. We'd found several giant pickle crocks in which to toss the salad; Clare magically produced paring knives and reappropriated hem rippers to scrape carrots, and we went at it as if we'd been fed only lunar-module food all summer.

Gary, the Tucson undergrad from the scene shop, had the brilliant idea of pouring wine into Welch's grape juice bottles so that we might dine out back of the theatre in a daring, Camp Frowns and Freaks If Camp Only Knew fashion. It was a simply swell afternoon of contraband wine, bio-real food, and the entire extended theatre family present and accounted for.

By the season's close, truth is, we ended up with two summer romances. Scott and Babs, two college-age staff members, who in early weeks of camp had seemed shy and uncomfortable, suddenly blossomed. Gary, the sweet, innocent charmer from Arizona (and a third holdout in the mustache retention program), ended up going with a grad student named Carol, the speech instructor, who was sarcastic, funny, and a tad dark. She seemed an odd match for Gary, but we liked her a lot and they, too, added a glow to our group.

Bob had a few admirers, too. In fact, most of the costume gals had their eye on him, and one was briefly in his company. In the end, though, Bob seemed to feel as free and indisposed to entanglements as did Susie and I. Perhaps there was an unconscious solidarity among our infamous trio. For myself, I felt immune to any real crushes; ultimately, the summer was about the pleasure of so many easy, uncomplicated friendships.

For the afternoon's big lunch party, everyone was draped on the grassy slope behind the theatre in the sun, eating, laughing, within view of Lake Wahbekanetta. From around the back corner of the theatre came Lisa, my stage-managing student, accompanied by another high schooler.

"Hey!" she shouted, doing a meek little hand wave.

"Ho," I answered.

"What are you guys doing? Is this the theatre staff picnic or something?" Lisa asked.

"Sort of. Nothing official, we just couldn't stand not having garlic and real vegetables—and dealing with one more dining hall meal," I answered, smiling while instinctively covering my plastic glass of grape juice with one hand.

"Ah," she nodded.

Lisa was a smart kid; Susie and I both thought so. Certain kids that age are mature enough that they sense, to an amazing degree, what is going on with adults, and they glide along making clever use of their insider knowledge.

"So how has your summer been, Lisa?" asked Susie.

"Really good. I liked hanging out here in High School Drama a lot more than girls' camp, though." Lisa gave us a funny look.

"Hmm, right," I said. "You mean like...?"

"I mean, we still have two weeks left of camp, and some of the girls in my cabin are already worrying about when to start crying at the final concert. Like you plan that all out," Lisa snickered, rolling her eyes. "And a couple of girls are worried they'll be in trouble when they turn in their uniforms, 'cause they messed with them a little."

"Some of them pegged them, huh?" I said, with a sly smile.

"How do *you* know about that?" said Lisa, her mouth open, braces flashing.

"Mmm. I have my ways, Lisa," I answered, smirking. I was enjoying holding out on her.

"What are you talking about?" Susie demanded. Lisa smiled and looked back at me.

"Well, some girls feel funny about their knickers not fitting well, especially the really ancient ones. So they end up finding navy thread and sewing darts to fit them better, so they don't look like — like Renaissance pages," I explained.

Susie laughed, shaking her head at Lisa. Lisa kept nodding, still a little rankled that I knew about this one.

"Anyway, they're all fine and everything," said Lisa. "I just feel more at home around the drama majors and you guys."

Years later, I thought about Lisa. I'm sure I identified

with her because she was the lone theatre-tech person,
wanting to stage-manage and not act. Neither she nor I
wanted to be the spear carrier; we wanted to be the spear
maker. Susie and I both wondered if Lisa would end up
going into theatre later on. She was bright and funny, and
had a wonderful sense around people. She could have just as
easily run a heroic nonprofit social services agency as been
in theatre.

Lisa started to take off, not speaking, but smiling and
doing her little wave.

"But wait," she said suddenly and turned back. "How
come you guys are all hanging out together on your day off?
Boy, you must really like each other a lot!"

"Yeah," I said. "We do."

And we smiled at one another, Lisa shooting me a last
look that seemed to indicate "Noted."

THE NERVE CENTER OF OPERATIONS for both camp
and the academy was the Maddy Building, a beautiful,
venerable native architecture structure composed of a
low, sloped, shingled roof, pine framing, and local stones.
Campers would pop in over the course of the summer to
withdraw small amounts of cash from their accounts, using
a sort of countdown punch card, in order to have pin money
for personal items.

Back in camper summers, my friend Barry and I used to
laugh about this because whenever we went in, we'd always
have to face a very stern redheaded woman at the teller

window. No matter how much we were withdrawing, she'd pause, look at us from her bifocals with beaded lanyard chains, and inquire, "Why so much?"

Who was she? Could she be the watchdog assistant to Maddy himself? In order to withdraw $10 the incorrect answer would be "Well, I want to treat my friends to banana splits at the Melody Freeze and get this neat T-shirt I saw in the campus store." Whereas the correct response might be "The music store has a paperbound copy of Artur Schnabel's edition of Beethoven's sonatas on sale, and my piano teacher thinks it's a pretty good deal."

Barry was such a good actor-liar that he'd always be able to get the ice cream and clothes, while I still have my two-volume set of Beethoven's thirty-two, but we loved teasing each other about going to visit the Why-So-Much-Lady, making her into a sort of Ernestine of the Phone Company in all her matriarchal camp fierceness.

CAMP GOT VERY QUIET after 9 p.m., but not everyone on staff wanted to retire to their cabins and read or drift off. A certain crew would head over to the ground level of the Maddy Building, to the wood-paneled staff lounge. The room had a comforting clubhouse feel; there would be a few smokers, some card players, and those who needed the stimulation of grown-up conversation.

One of the regulars there was Jay, a staging assistant and aspiring opera director. He was a gregarious East Coaster, and hanging out there provided him with an essential connection to the big-city culture peers (i.e., other East Coasters) that he'd quickly spotted during his northern Michigan summer hiatus. He would hold court there, discussing why Sondheim could never be a match for Gershwin, gesturing and getting excited; Bob would mutter to me under his breath, "There's Jay at it again. What's with the puppet show?"

One night, Bob and I wandered over to the Maddy. I plopped into a low, soft-cushioned tubular aluminum chair, feeling satisfied and more in the mood to hang than to enter into any animated powwow. Gossip per se was pretty rare, but once in a while one might stumble into something.

Two regulars at the lounge were John and Vicky, exact opposites who'd often spar if anyone let them get into it. Vicky worked at camp and was the know-it-all daughter of a veteran administrator. She was smart and a little tiresome in large doses. John was a jock who had something to do with the university division; for him, the primary appeal of Interlochen was its very favorable gal-to-guy ratio.

John was already seated in the lounge when Vicky came in and sat down a few seats away. "Hey there, Vicky. How's it hanging?" he said, in his usual clumsy fashion.

"Fine. Just the usual end-of-season hysteria stuff," she said disinterestedly.

"So Vick-eeey...I have to a-s-k you something. Were you up late last night?"

"Yeah, I guess. I don't remember."

"Isn't your cabin over by the visitor parking lots, just beyond Giddings Concourse?"

"So? What—are you spying on staff women these days?" Vicky was already getting huffy, exactly the reaction John seemed to be pushing for.

"Well, so...didn't I see you wandering around near the highway entrance last night...at 11:30 or 12...in your *nightgown*?" John asked, grinning and greedy with his loaded question.

Vicky said nothing and shrugged. The room was dimly lit, but it did seem as though some color came into her face.

"WOAH. Hahahaha! There we GO! What do we have here...the hot sleepwalker of Interlochen?! *Woo-wheee!*" John couldn't contain himself.

Vicky stood up and drifted to the other end of the lounge. I looked at Bob. No way did either of us want to be at all complicit in John's little discovery, so we avoided eye contact with him. Clearly the best move was to grab that one late-night-snack opportunity at the food-counter window—where they served sodas, ice cream, and the best toasted English muffins (from Bay's in Chicago). Then to bed. The big, familiar finale was almost upon us.

Liszt Is More

THE SUMMER WAS INDEED drawing to a close; I half expected to see "Final Week!" banners in front of all the performance spaces on campus. The end of the season was even more hectic than the first few days, and the center of campus was thick with parents, tourists, and concertgoers. A sure sign that the season was in its final days was the long lines forming at the Melody Freeze, camp's one concession to sin, serving soft ice cream.

The mood was upbeat and anxious, full of bittersweet anticipation of it all ending soon, including so many fused-at-the-hip friendships, as campers were about to return to California, Virginia, Maine, Puerto Rico, Germany, France, or wherever else they called home.

High School Drama was heading into its final production—*As You Like It*, for which we'd unfurled our ragtag Old Globe Theatre–style banners and strung them on poles in front of Grunow. In off moments we were getting a jump on writing camper evaluations, packing things into winter storage, and working in as many more free-for-all falls with our pals as time would allow. It hit me; I couldn't believe we were living a temporary existence, eight little weeks of summer. I was no longer a camper, but it had been impossible not to be swept away once again, in this real-life movie musical we were in.

It's funny how, if you're ensconced somewhere far from home and the going is good, you have no difficulty whatsoever giving up your possessions, driving a car, being with your closest friends and family, and worrying about all your troubles. It's easier, of course, if you're young and unattached and still free enough to let go. At one point several of us admitted to each other that we were being paid the huge sum of $250 for the entire summer. But with meals provided and little time to shop or head into town, we were returning home with cash left over. It was absurd, poetic simplicity.

It would be easy to imagine that the high school musical or the operetta would be the summer's main theatrical attraction for audiences and performers. But it wasn't quite like that. The play's the thing...as it turned out...to show off the full range of talent and winning ways of each summer's merry band of high school thespians. Brian, the director, had the honor of being the last one up, and even though his choice of Shakespeare was one of the comedies, it proved more challenging than the other productions to rehearse and to ignite into performance.

One night, I remember a preperformance tableaux in back of Grunow during the half hour before the show was to begin. August meant a lot more heat was building up inside the theatre, especially backstage and in the light mirror–bejeweled dressing rooms. So we all agreed to allow the cast to get some air behind the building, as long as they remained concealed from the audiences filing in for the performance.

Susie was on call as the wardrobe assistant that night, in case a button popped off or a fabric tear needed immediate repair. She and I were standing outside watching the cast warming up, getting out their last bits of excess nervous energy. The sun was still setting late by mid-August, casting a low-angled flood of caramel-colored light onto the actors' faces and costumes. They were in almost complete silhouette against the sky, so we were watching the outlines of their figures in tights, tunics, Elizabethan neck ruffles, and long sweeping skirts—all horsing around like wind-up Shakespearean comedy action figures. The effect was beautiful and comic at the same time. They were enjoying each other and delighting in anachronistically singing snips from *The Music Man* or doing vaudeville slapstick moves from their favorite old movies.

"Aren't they just a riot?" Susie said, amid her sniff-giggles.

"Clowning right up to the very last. It's classic."

Brian appeared, looking as tall and high-spirited as ever. He walked around to the various groupings of actors to say "Break a leg," then came toward us, looking pleased and relaxed.

"Brian...it's a great show, congrats," I said to him.

"Really, Brian. They're wonderful, and the actors adore you," said Susie.

Brian smiled and laughed, "Well, it's good to see they're finally having some fun."

Susie lowered her voice a little and said, "Look at Alexis in her Audrey wench costume, hands on her hips, really getting into it—that would be me, in my first role in high school. There weren't that many girls who could fill in the costume." She puckered her lips and struck a baby-doll pose, her eyes rolled all the way up.

Without losing a beat, Brian mirrored Susie's facial expression in a sort of campy Robin Williams equivalent. He launching into a limerick, speaking slowly enough to give him time to compose it on the fly.

> *There once was a redhead named Sus - an,*
> *Who really had quite a nice bos - om.*
> *Her blouse was quite tight,*
> *Her knickers just right,*
> *It's easy to see how she woos 'em!*

"Brian, you are such a nut!" I said, while Susie hissed and laughed, looking flattered.

Lisa, the student stage manager in charge, was making the rounds to let everyone know it was "Five minutes till curtain!" The actors scooped up their long, bulky costumes and bustled their way up the wooden steps to the backstage doors.

"I've had a very good summer," Brian began, "not without a few funny situations—but really, they're all so fresh, so willing. It's a lovely break from college students, who can be a little hardboiled at times. So self-conscious about everything before they even try."

"How did you ever get them to stop doing the British accents?" asked Susie.

"Ha. You mean the thirty versions of *Masterpiece Theatre* English?" he said. "That took a week or so to dismantle. I was surprised, though—in the end they even managed to shed all those New York, Chicago, Texas accents."

"I wondered about that. But some of them are very determined."

"After all that, I was looking to see how they'd find their way into the play," Brian said, folding his arms and trying not to sound too professorial. "At some point they get over being so deathly afraid of Shakespeare, and they start to see their characters as just…their mean next-door neighbor, a drunken uncle, or a lovelorn friend at school."

"And then they figure out how to *sell it*…."

"Exactly," Brian said. "It's even better, because they're able to put it across onstage to kids their own age, really. That's not so easy."

"Sweet," said Susie, simply.

"Well, shall we?" I said. It was on to the 302nd performance of the forty-fifth season. We followed the little Shakespeareans into the smallest Old Globe ever to feel the heat, hear the words, see the wench, and get a bit of the Bard's magic once more.

CAMP BUILDS FOR THE BIG MOMENT—every year on the final night of camp, an ensemble of more than four hundred performs a melodramatic whomper of a symphonic tone poem, Franz Liszt's *Les Preludes*. The thematic camp connection was that for a student of life and art, somehow the end is really just the beginning. I think Maddy liked closing each summer with a big showpiece that was stirring and ultraromantic, in order to seal the emotional bond—as well as to be able to stage a performance that could incorporate an unlimited number of performers, like Mahler's "Symphony of a Thousand."

The Interlochen Bowl, where the final concert was held, was built in time for the first season of camp in 1928, seating, at the time, an astounding eight thousand. My small, worn Interlochen songbook shows *Les Preludes* on the cover in all its splendor and histrionics. The concert made use of as many instrumentalists, singers, and dancers as could fit onto (and in front of) the stage. Only the drama kids got off the hook.

The songbook's cover photo of the concert, taken in the mid-'50s, is so over the top that you could swear that what you're looking at is all retoucher's magic. Rows of harpists. Every string, brass, piccolo, Sousaphone player. Every possible chorister. Female dancers frame the stage in front, wearing red- or blue-paneled tunic dresses, doing penché or heavenward poses in the unmistakable angular style of Martha Graham. Another dozen, clad in gauzy pink gowns, walk slowly on the roof of the Bowl during the final measures of music. Dancers hold the edges of a large diaphanous white

cloth and raise it up suddenly to catch the air, bunching it in to form a balloon shape before returning it again to the rooftop.

My songbook was a hand-me-down from another camper; on the cover photo, someone has used a blue ballpoint pen to scratch in a church cross at the roof's peak, which the dancers in the photo are seemingly drawn to: a boy-camper editorial touch, probably intended as much as a jab at Liszt as at the camp pageantry itself. Was it a religious ceremony? A Cecil B. DeMille production? A graduation ceremony out of control? It was all of these things. Even an eight-year-old understood that this was one big, overly trumped-up production number. But it was a gas to be in it, watch it, and even attend it more than once. No experience was more Interlochen than *Les Preludes.*

The three of us—Susie, Bob, and I—sat together in the audience for the ritual conclusion of the summer of '72, thought-cloud balloons floating over our heads containing variations on *This really is it, the final night. Tomorrow is 'So long.'*

Waiting for the final concert to begin, feeling a short but wild chapter of my life drawing to a close, I wondered for the first time what would become of our group. At that moment I couldn't have known that we would continue in careers as actors, directors, costumers, scene painters, designers, and teachers—and that nearly a dozen of us would keep in touch by means of Interlochen's invisible web of shared experience.

I'd lose track of one or two, and then they would turn up again. Bob resurfaced as a cameraman for public television, Clare as a theatre professor. After grad school Susie worked as an actress for several years before marrying an actor and raising a son who was well on his way to life as a stage performer when she settled into her next career, as surely one of the most magnetic primary-school teachers in New York City.

And for myself...I did not imagine that my own travels would include working as a puppeteer, artist, textile designer, teacher, and ballet-company musician, and would lead eventually to a profession as an art director/graphic designer in solo practice. This touchstone summer would be, as it turned out, the start of a life in which I wouldn't have to have a second "day job" to support my creative pursuits; I would always be in the arts, and would invariably align myself with others who had real passion for what they were doing.

"TOUCH THAT," whispered Susie, pinching her knickers' corduroy at the knee and placing my hand on the fabric.

"Huh?" I said.

"They're mine. These knickers are now my own. I bought them," she said proudly.

It had happened. Year after year, strange as it always seemed, many girls and grown women ended up buying their own knickers because they had fallen in love with them, for whatever reason—for their comfort, for their memories, or as boywear antifashion statement. This despite our unconfirmed suspicion that the knickers were chosen because they were unflattering to adolescent girls—and that light blue stockings were chosen for high schoolers because they somehow made calves seem fatter. Outsiders never quite believed that anyone would purchase the knickers. But every year, they did....And I suppose the uniforms office just had to order more for the following summer.

Sitting and waiting in those last few moments for *Les Preludes* to begin, my mind drifted back to my first camper summer. I had walked down a long series of wooden steps to Dr. and Mrs. Maddy's lakeside residence cabin for cookies and lemonade. Every camper was invited to meet them personally at some point during the course of the summer. At fifteen, I didn't know enough to understand what a pioneer and visionary Joseph Maddy had been—that he was a true risk-taker, a convincer, driven to somehow find support, even during the Depression, to realize this big dream. A dream that would unfold with an energy and design all its own.

Even then, at the age of seventy-four, he was still shaking campers' hands and smiling—sporting his famous Milo O'Shea eyebrows. Both Maddys were very sweet, but I think Mrs. Maddy might have scored more points with the girls if she'd worn knickers instead of the dignified faculty-staff option of the A-line corduroy skirt and blouse.

When I was leaving their cabin along with a dozen other boys, I kept thinking of a joke, a Tom Swiftie that was all the rage that summer: "'There will be no *Les Preludes* this year,' said Dr. Maddy, Liszt-lessly."

In reality, the summer of 1965 was to be Maddy's last time at the podium as conductor; he passed away the following spring.

THE CLOSING CONCERT, in all its stagy Wagnerian proportions, ended, and with it came the summer's final playing of the Interlochen Theme. If you knew to squint and watch for it, you would see that after lowering the baton for the final note, the conductor snapped the baton in two and tossed the pieces to the musicians, a little ritual symbol of camp closure.

The sky had darkened to a deep Creamsicle glow by the end of the performance, and there were more pairs of corduroys in one place than at any other event of the season. All at once, bodies were weaving their way out of the Bowl like hundreds of dark blue pipe cleaners carefully untangling from a tube; you could practically hear the rubbing of corduroy-encased legs, as well as the countless number of tearful farewells already beginning.

The next morning, campers, staff, and faculty rose early to meet parents, cars, buses, and planes to disassemble our own short-lived piece of performance art, Interlochen Summer of '72.

A little crew from the theatre staff had breakfast together

the last morning. At that precise moment probably all of us would have said we would return the next summer, and many did. Bob had to leave the earliest, saying his short, smiling good-bye, with hugs all around in what should have been a perfect model for the rest of us later on.

Three parties took off at the same time. Susie was traveling with a San Diego carful. I was hopping a ride to Detroit with Carol, the speech instructor and Gary's summer romance. And Gary rode with a group in a third car in the exit convoy.

We drove out onto the highway and came to a Y in the road. Susie's and Gary's cars veered onto the left highway, and Carol's and mine to the right: a gentle break, not a snap, of the wishbone. It was as if I were watching the choreographed car moves in the final, aerial shot of a movie.

The Interlochen summer had been like the rush from a wild amusement-park ride. I felt as though I had to consciously release myself from its built-up gravitational pull in order to head home and start the next phase of my life, a twenty-two-year-old's fresh slate on which to begin.

Rewind to the Shrine

OVER THE NEXT THIRTY-ODD YEARS, Interlochen would weave in and out of my consciousness with a quietly sustained presence. Often I'd meet people professionally in the music, dance, or art/design worlds and learn, much later on, by chance, that they had also been to Interlochen. In addition to keeping friendships from my high school and staff days, I made new friends with others who had lived complementary versions of the Interlochen experience.

One of those friends, Joan, was especially loyal to both camp and the academy, and she managed regular pilgrimages to Michigan every few years. Before each visit she would urge me to come along; I'd be torn because I was broke, felt pressed for time, or had some other sad little excuse. But I would grill her thoroughly after her visits. Clearly, a persistent curiosity was nagging away at me.

By the time I sat down to reconstruct my own summers on paper, Joan's timing was, at last, perfect: she could see even better than I that in order to put the finishing touch on my thoughts, I needed to go for a visit. Without even a hint of tongue in cheek or sarcasm, she wrote me that a return to camp would unquestionably be "a life-changing experience" and asked what I was waiting for. What the heck—Joan was prepared to haul out from New Jersey, so I could certainly do so from Seattle.

Hastily, happily, I cranked into gear putting a visit together—in the nick of time, as I quickly discovered that camp's season had just changed to six weeks in place of the traditional eight. My anticipation and excitement level surprised even me...and off I went, prepared for four days of wandering between Lakes Wahbekanetta and Wahbekaness.

Even on the red-eye from Seattle to Detroit, questions were gathering inside me with surprising emotional intensity and suspense. How dramatically had Interlochen changed? Was the sense of spirit and camaraderie still strong and palpable? Would it still feel like a boot camp for the arts, where rules were in full force? I needed to know if there was still the heightened sense of activity— and, basically, if Interlochen *could still do it*. Armed with a (greatly expanded) campus map and my questions, I was off to explore and match up impressions of camp that were thirty-three years apart.

IMMEDIATELY UPON ARRIVING IN TRAVERSE CITY, I tore out of the airport, driving directly to camp, sunshine and curiosity streaming down in full force. Stepping out of the rental car, I opened the trunk, pulled out my backpack, and for a split second thought to myself, "What *exactly* am I doing here?" I felt a flash of momentary insanity in being past the point of no return, wondering what was drawing me to be here at camp after what seemed like about a hundred years. I smiled, slammed the trunk, and scooted across the parking lot to the epicenter of campus.

At first glance, everything appeared strikingly the same. Only the trees and shrubs had grown spectacularly, lush and laden, like a set for a French grand opera set in the wilds of Michigan. One thing that hit me right away, however, was that the campers looked relaxed, almost breezy—and they were in various groups of boys and girls together, *playing Ping-Pong at the center of camp*. I nearly started laughing; the image was decidedly unlike any of those '60s brochures. Granted, the pressure was off campers during the last few days of the season, but I hadn't realized until that moment how polarized the sexes were during my camp years.

Just prior to my visit, I learned that there had been one other notable camp change: knickers were now required only as concert dress. In recent years, non-corduroy pants and shorts options had been introduced for both girls and boys. And yet corduroy knickers were still worn voluntarily by a sizable contingent of girls, who had perfected an updated, slouchier way to wear them—with knee flaps unbuttoned, the garment hanging straight down loosely,

hip-hop style. A few minutes earlier, the last thing my new friends Jenny and Judy at the information booth had yelled after me as I went on to explore camp was "We LOVE our knickers!" So I wasn't on Mars; some things had persisted.

One of the first things I did was walk up to the entrance of Kresge Auditorium, where an orchestra was rehearsing a 1920s jazz-inspired symphonic piece by Milhaud. The woman standing next to me had a knowing grin on her face that seemed, ironically, to mirror my own.

"God," I said to her, "I had forgotten how beautiful the ripples of the lake are through the windows at the back of the stage, standing from here."

"Yes, it's just spellbinding, isn't it?" the woman immediately responded in a clipped upstate New York accent.

"Are you here visiting your kids at camp, or...?" I asked.

"No, no. I tagged along with a friend whose kids are here. I just wanted to make the trek and see camp again." She smiled.

A little jolt of bonding and recognition leapt between us. The woman was making a return visit for herself, just as I was. We smiled, and she was off to join her friend. I stood there, immobilized, for another moment. It was sunny, forty international flags were flying overhead, and the scene was completed by a lake breeze and the seductive live symphonic music. I had walked back into a movie and was home once again.

The visit was overwhelming. I wouldn't have dreamed I would find the spirit and essence of the place so intact, at least from my impressions in four days of wandering around. Easily enough, I found myself talking with forty or fifty people on campus, all told—parents, campers, staff, faculty, and alumni—from music librarians to High School Drama majors to choral teaching assistants and counselors.

Parents, many of whom were campers themselves in the '60s or '70s, were especially effusive and candid with me about their impressions of camp. One pair of parents laughingly said they'd arrived at camp a day or two ago, but their three boys didn't have all that much time for them. A single father and music teacher confessed that he dreamed of working there for a summer, and wondered if he would make the cut as faculty. A parent from Chicago remarked upon the wonderful change in his daughter at camp as well as his chagrin that she phoned him every day to share her excitement.

These days, high school and even elementary school kids are so adult as well as so techno-enabled that I half expected to see campers w a l k i n g about heavily accessorized,

with cell phones, earpieces, and laptops instead of ice cream cones, cello cases, and practice batons.

Camp had come right out and banned cell phones. Although parents pushed back (and these days, they are actually the ones who balk, bitch, and moan about any rule they interpret as restrictive or abusive), the policy seemed to have stuck. The camp line was that for this short six-week camp season, the goal is for kids to have maximum face-to-face time with other campers and their teachers. Admittedly, I did get some satisfaction from watching an irritated corporate-type dad having trouble with cell phone reception—in northern woods that he might have been better off appreciating for their lovely remoteness.

I was guessing, from the more relaxed appearance of the campers—which seemed a positive, subtle change from my own summers—that the kids were wise enough to grasp what Interlochen is really all about. That this remote, unusual place wasn't anything like their hometown, wherever that might be. I had to admit that there seemed to be a new and fitting sense of balance. Things had evolved.

I couldn't resist asking campers if they thought there were too many rules. One high school girl paused, then replied, "Not overly." Another camper told me, "Yeah...but it's okay." Two high school boys offered that campers still had to get up at 6:30 for reveille, but it seemed more like bragging than complaining. The sheer challenge of in-your-face discipline is really an attraction to young artists, who are learning to what degree they are committed to it all. It was still a boot camp, after all. Or a "summer intensive," as people say nowadays.

The visit, after so many years away, was filled with all sorts of missions and burning questions. I was flying all around camp as if I were on a timed scavenger hunt. It was a treasure hunt, too.

The woman standing with me at Kresge when I first arrived had clued me in on the Apollo alumni house, at the center of camp. Inside, it was a fairy-tale-perfect Beatrix Potter stone cottage complete with the low embers of a fire in the wood-burning fireplace, homespun rockers, old camp photos and programs everywhere, and a friendly volunteer — a living shrine poised to welcome alumni looking to connect again and confirm that it had all been real.

Not far from the alumni house was the photo archive, which seemed, miraculously, to possess every official photo from camp's earliest years to the current closing week. It was a veritable Library of Congress of Interlochen, with hundreds of carefully labeled boxes storing photos of music performances, plays, musicals, operettas, cabin groupings, and even posed shots of girls smiling while working out those delicate negotiations at the uniforms office. I found photos of Susie and Brian in *Charlie Brown*, and one in which I was glumly posing with the boys of Cabin 11 hoping for some good news. A camp official told me that families donate, with some regularity, shoeboxes of childhood camp photos — as if every possible moment weren't already carefully documented and preserved.

Also at the center of camp is the Stone Center, which houses the dining hall and a hotel for visitors. I remembered that as campers we weren't supposed to go into the hotel lobby, but we lingered there anyway, on the pretense of visiting parents, because it had a homey lodge feeling that we sought on rainy days.

During this visit I was staying at camp, so I had a chance to look over the hotel lobby with a fresh, closer eye. It was comforting that very little had changed, but my selective vision focused on a few details.

Some things that had always been in the lobby, but that now called anew to me, were the original photos of camp from the '20s and '30s. The wide, panoramic shots were taken with a camera that rotated in a slow arc and depended on the assistance of patient, cooperative sitters—all seven or eight thousand of them—in the Interlochen Bowl. I'd have paid someone to sneak one of those photos out of there and into my suitcase.

The other curiosity in the lobby was the oil painting of longtime camp supporter W. Clement Stone and his wife, Jessie. The hotel and a theatre-gymnasium on campus were named for them. A friend who attended the winter academy had told me that Stone would haul out his checkbook every year and ask Joseph Maddy how much money he needed to keep things afloat. Stone himself was quite a figure—a Chicago millionaire businessman, philanthropist, and self-help book author. His can-do philosophy perfectly complemented the Maddy determination.

I stared at the double portrait. Its lurid, surreal style seemed somewhere between a Dali portrait and a velvet painting, with Stone and his famous pencil-thin black mustache and polka-dot bow tie, and Jessie towering next to him in a riotously printed dress. I almost expected a motion-activated voice to boom out with advice on achieving success through a positive mental attitude.

There had been just enough time for me to take a quick hike to the High School Boys division, noting as I did that the footpaths had been slightly rerouted to avoid passing by the All-State cabins altogether. One of the tennis courts was taken up with a large fallen branch that had evidently been there for some time; I was glad to see that the arts still triumphed over sports.

On my way back to the main campus, I overheard a camper father with a Belgian accent asking his son if he needed any help in packing. His son replied blandly, "Nah, not really. All I have to pack is a flashlight and a couple of iPods."

My visit wouldn't have been complete without seeing Grunow to find out if there were any ghosts of Susie, Bob, and the others. Surprisingly, the building looked very much the same, although it was being used only for music rehearsals now. A peek through the windows of the locked basement allowed me a view of the same cinderblock room that had been the scene of so much laughter and carryings-on during my staff summer.

On the back door of Grunow was posted a laser-printed sign that read

> *By divine decree from the Lord High Executioner*
> *this is now a* SHOE-FREE ZONE

showing that at least a bit of the mischievous elfin-camper

quality I'd enjoyed at camp was still alive.

It was even more reassuring because, as I soon learned, the great Interlochen summer operetta tradition had come to a halt the very summer of my return visit. After seventy-five years or so... why? I was aghast and disheartened. Dear old Gilbert and Sullivan: the operettas' buoyant burlesque, their disarming tunefulness, and the sheer brilliance of those clever, Oscar Wilde–imprinted lyrics. I'd never fully understood why G&S seemed so unappreciated and marginalized in this country, although the operettas still manage to keep semi- or nonprofessional troupes ("societies") alive in various cities.

But as a concert- and performancegoer, I'd realized that operettas weren't, as a rule, popular with either musical-comedy fans or opera lovers—who were thought to have gone soft if they admitted to liking Gilbert and Sullivan. Only a few years ago, the venerable D'Oyly Carte Opera Company, which had been performing the operettas from their inception, went into hibernation. The company website is still online, complete with cast lists and details of past productions, but no other vital signs remain.

Upon reflection, it seemed rather amazing that operetta had persisted so long at camp, especially as kids' lives had gotten faster and full of the need for a different sort of musical theatre and performance altogether. Campers today might have bop, Bartok, or Buxtehude on their iPods; they're less likely to have *H.M.S. Pinafore* or *Princess Ida* in their playlists. Perhaps over the years the camp operetta was merely tolerated, like *Les Preludes*—a set piece that was simply one of the familiar milestones of a summer racing by.

Was this all true? I was a little saddened until several staff on campus lowered their voices and said things like "Mmm, maybe. It doesn't mean operetta won't be back, you know." There were even rumors of a knickers/cords-only sing-along version scheduled for the following summer. *Interesting,* I thought to myself, feeling hopeful.

Music and musical tastes follow a pendulum that moves back and forth at its own strange pace. When something is dowdy and down and out for a long time, it can suddenly reappear: brighter, untouched, and appreciated anew. Perhaps camp could survive on a diet of *Show Boat* and *Sweeney Todd* for a few more years before *The Mikado* and *The Pirates of Penzance* would return, more gorgeous and winning than ever.

Several uncanny coincidences and reconnections happened during my four days. I was glad, for one, to get a chance to chat with a delightful alumna volunteer in her late seventies who was a source of rich detail on aspects of camp history. Since I didn't really know Joseph Maddy personally—and she did—I was glad to clear something up that had always puzzled me. Accounts I'd read of Maddy portrayed him as a visionary with clear ideas and a strong will. But whether he was really a curmudgeon, I never was sure. She was firm in setting the record straight: "Joseph Maddy was not crotchety! Not at all. He loved those kids."

LUCKILY, I DID MANAGE to meet up with Dude briefly
on two occasions during my visit. By this time he'd been
teaching at Interlochen continuously since 1953. There he
was, at seventy-seven, dashing at top speed in the direction
of the dining hall; when he saw me, we stopped to chat a
little about the summer ending and the bare outlines of our
own lives.

"Dude, remember that I was here in the dim dark
ages . . . when the high school productions were still being
put on in Grunow!" I said to him.

"Oh *well* . . . I'll tell you," he paused and turned his head
at an angle, "sometimes I think everything looked even better
on that little stage, shows exploding with energy . . . you
know?"

"So you're not too upset about no big operetta for the
first time this summer?" I asked.

"Naw, no . . . it's fine. They'd really gotten very expensive,
you know," he said softly, looking silently amused.

"I guess it's not as if you *needed* to do another one after
all these years." I looked down for a moment, then finally got
up the nerve to broach a different topic. "Dude, I've decided
I want to write it all down, my summers here. See if I can
capture any of it," I said. "Of course, you're in there, along
with Susie and the rest of the group from '72."

"Oh, let the past be in the past!" Dude said, shaking his
head and wrinkling his face. Then he brightened, adding,
"Well, say whatever you want about me!" He laughed and
started to head back toward the dining hall. Then, quite out
of the blue, he turned back and added, "You know, nobody

could raise money like Joseph Maddy. Nobody even came close."

MY VISIT CLOSED WITH — what else but *Les Preludes*. The audience seemed to be drawn from everywhere and every social strata. Elderly locals had bicycled to camp on their three-speeds with front straw baskets; there were stylish moms from Long Island with power haircuts; and seated behind me was the ten-year veteran postmaster of the town of Interlochen itself.

After the first half of the program, the World Youth Symphony had to undergo its transformation into a 450-piece ensemble. It was easy to forget that this is no simple feat; it takes twenty or twenty-five minutes simply to fill up the Bowl's jumbo-sized candy box with musicians. Sections were called out one by one in the eloquent diction of an acting student: "Violas B3, enter stage right please. Brass J4, enter left now. Will the orchestra members please try to refrain from making noise—and members of the audience as well, thank you." Most of the audience was standing, fascinated to watch this half-time show and find out exactly how these armies would all fit into this amazing tightly packed space.

With my camp curiosity on overdrive for the last few days, I must have seemed to have a sign on my forehead warning people that I was from NPR and I had to know *everything*. But *Les Preludes* is a family affair; everyone was chatting freely to one another as we waited in our seats at intermission.

"Did you have a good summer?" I asked the two women in their twenties to my right.

"Yeah," answered one, "it's been fun. We're both choral coaches for Intermediates."

"And were they a handful? Did anything...especially funny happen over the course of the summer?"

"Mmm. Not really," one woman answered. She thought a bit more, then continued, "Well, we did have one girl from an Eastern European country who didn't know very much English. But one of the campers kind of helped work it out."

"You mean she knew the language, was able to act as interpreter?" I asked.

"No, that's the thing. I would say something like 'I want you to play an A-major scale slowly and evenly,'" she explained, "and the other girl would repeat to her what I'd said, but with an accent, scrambling the word order of the sentence. And it just...kind of worked!"

"Ha," I nodded, returning her smile.

"I think the other thing was something another staff member told me. One of the Intermediate boys, a saxophone player, broke his finger during the first few days and had to go home. One of the other boys told his teacher, 'The whole cabin has been crying all week, but we've stopped now. Finally, we realized we had to somehow go on with our lives.' Odd, right? I mean, boys that age aren't usually all that keen on showing their emotions!"

We both laughed, and one of the two men in front of us turned and interjected, "Well, if you think about it—a certain part of Interlochen is about the crying."

The postmaster behind me tapped my shoulder, leaned forward, and added, "Even *I* could have told you that!"

There were six or seven of us laughing together by this time; I then asked one of the two men in front of me, "Were you guys on staff, too, this summer? You seem to know the drill."

"No—just visiting from the Bay Area, up here for a family wedding, and I had to bring my partner to see camp," he said.

"He's heard quite enough about it over the last few years, then, huh?" I said.

"Oh yeah," he answered, chuckling, while his partner nodded and produced a mock injured-party face.

"Well, I guess *Preludes* would have to be the perfect rite of initiation then," I said.

"Uh-huh," he answered. "I haven't been here since I was at the academy. Things have changed here and there."

"But . . . it's good?" I asked.

"Yeah . . . well, you know," he answered. "It'll always be Interlochen. Thank God!"

The ensemble onstage had finished tuning all the instrumental sections and was quieting down as the audience settled in for the performance. A minute before it all began, a black squirrel skittered atop the roof of the Bowl's stage. I was trying to remember if the opening notes of the Liszt began with a boom, and would the squirrel jump directly upward? But the little preshow performer scooted off onto a nearby pine bough moments before the music began; no doubt he'd been there for many summers, and was trained to make room for the dancers already on their way up to perform there.

One other woodland/woodwind touch segued into the actual downbeat of the orchestra. From a few hundred yards away came the scales of a clarinetist at practice. I wasn't the only one who chuckled softly; it was if the young musician had secretly and defiantly said to himself that morning, "I've played in enough *Preludes*. I'm going home tomorrow, and I want to practice, and that's all there is to it!" A staff woman in a corduroy skirt frowned in horror and set off running at top speed in the direction of the practice huts as the unstoppable, monster spectacle began.

WITH THE PASSING OF SO MANY YEARS, the various twists, turns, and iterations of my own life in art and design have left me with altered, clearer insights on what Interlochen has ultimately meant to me and perhaps to others.

For years I'd always assumed it was my family that fostered my habits of focus, intensity, and the desire to seek and invent—aspects of obsessive-compulsive behavior that an artist or designer needs to get on with it. Or I considered them the real takeaway from art school, populated as it is with its own array of devilish taskmaster professors.

But the truth is, I really observed these qualities and was compelled to adopt them first at Interlochen, where I was exposed to the brightest and the most driven—who were not teachers or visiting celebrity artists, but kids my own age.

There was something else that was special about Interlochen, the aspect of kids observing grown-up versions of their own lives. It couldn't have been only my stage manager student, Lisa, who absorbed a view of adult working life that was one of positive possibility. What you do to make a living can, with a great deal of luck, be something that includes spirit, joyful collaboration, and real passion.

I never felt that Interlochen was anything like *Fame,* with all those predictable TV/movie plotlines and stock characters. Kids weren't running around madly seeking teachers who were (or had been) celebrated artists, nor were they spending time figuring out which fellow campers might "make it" in music, drama, dance, and so on.

Although it was impossible to ignore the roster of famous Interlochen alumni and faculty, the experience was really about soaking up the intensity of everything happening during a summer and returning home to translate some of it into the pattern puzzle of your own life, in all kinds of ways. You might not ever be able to explain the Interlochen mystique successfully to anyone later in life, but you carried something with you that was amazing and indelible.

Alumni who return to Interlochen are usually thought of as simply nostalgic, holding on to their semiprecious-jewel images of Interlochen as Oz or Brigadoon. But who can say how much is a recalling of youth, and how much is a return to find something else? A voyage back might be for closure...but it might also be for reopening a part of yourself that is still there—unflexed and obscured by life's ever-increasing clutter.

After this trip Joan wrote me, "I love going back to visit because it reminds me that I have to make the effort to create magic in real life . . . something that always seems to get lost in the shuffle." Well said, I thought. It surprised me that I'd returned home with nearly as many new stories as I had from my youthful summers. All told, I'd be hard put to think of a place where I had laughed and enjoyed the company of others quite so much.

After the performance of *Les Preludes* of this last visit, I had witnessed the campers' kiss-and-cry farewells, the group hugs, and the intensity of separation at the official closing of summer. The old sentiment that "by the end of camp, the kids don't really want to go home at all" seemed as true as ever. In spirit, not one thing had changed in forty years.

Then I had hiked down beneath Kresge, where staff and alumni were invited for a bonfire on the edge of Lake Wahbekanetta, adults and kids toasting marshmallows on sticks. A sunset ending that needed no additional swells of music.

When camp first opened in 1928, it was called National High School Orchestra Camp. In 1932 the name changed to National Music Camp; in 1990 it became Interlochen Arts Camp. The Interlochen Arts Academy opened in 1962 and still retains its original name. The Interlochen Center for the Arts was created in 1990 and today includes the camp; the academy; WIAA/ Interlochen Public Radio (IPR); Interlochen Pathfinder School, an independent day school; the College of Creative Arts, an adult education program; and year-round arts festivals.

Programs of study at Interlochen include music, art, theatre, dance, and creative writing; a motion picture arts program was added in 2005.

Interlochen Center for the Arts
www.interlochen.org

Interlochen Public Radio (IPR/WIAA)
www.interlochen.org/ipr/

BOOKS ON INTERLOCHEN

Joe Maddy of Interlochen: Profile of a Legend
Norma Lee Browning
Contemporary Books, 1992
ISBN 0-8092-3907-8

Interlochen: A Home for the Arts
Dean Boal
University of Michigan Press, 1998
ISBN 0-472-10882-4

Interlochen: Changing Lives for Seventy-Five Years
Text by Paul Heaton
Interlochen Center for the Arts, 2003
ISBN 0-9729428-0-7

ACKNOWLEDGMENTS

In putting together recollections of Interlochen, I have endeavored to capture my own account of the summers of 1965, 1966, and 1972. These are memories, subject to the frailties and tricks of the human mind, namely my own.

As camp's song suggests, alumni of Interlochen enjoy a "welcome you'll ever find"— and I am grateful to staff members for trusting me, manuscript unseen, to create a published piece that would contribute to the image of Interlochen in a positive way. My thanks to Lilias Circle, David Montee, Thom Paulson, and Kathleen Perez at Interlochen. I wish to thank, in particular, Paul Heaton for his gracious and responsive assistance.

Certainly, I owe a debt to the three previous books on Interlochen, especially Dean Boal's thorough and carefully researched history, *Interlochen: A   Home for the Arts.* Reacquainting myself with these books helped clarify some of my youthful, sketchy impressions about Joseph Maddy and camp history.

I would also like to express my appreciation to the following friends, who generously offered their own remembrances, cheering me on in my renewed excitement over camp: Jonathan Hollander, M.J. Kaplan, Pat Mullen, Matthew Nash, Kay Panterne, and most especially, Joan Pollack.

So many wonderful souls attended Interlochen with me and offered their friendship, humor, and spirit, for which I am forever indebted. My deepest admiration and respect goes to Clarence "Dude" Stephenson, who has touched the lives of countless students and colleagues over the last fifty-three years.

Fresh editorial insights and thoughtful suggestions were provided by two longtime friends, both of whom are wonderful writers: Judy Karasik and Ellen Pskowski. I'm also grateful for loyal help and support from John Berry, Eileen Gunn, Sherri Shultz, Jeff Slater, and Sarah Tyler.

Finally, I would like to thank my partner, Mike, for his artful, fresh eye and cheerful support during the writing, writhing, and rewriting of this past year.

— T F

THOM FEILD *has led a colorful career as a musician, artist, theatre craftsman, and graphic designer. He was a pianist with over a dozen dance companies, including American Ballet Theatre, Alvin Ailey Dance Theater, Washington Ballet, and New York Theatre Ballet. Thom has worked with Kennedy Center Productions and as a performer/craftsman with the Smithsonian Puppet Theatre.*

His work has been exhibited at the American Museum of Design and the Smithsonian's Renwick Gallery in Washington, as well as in galleries nationally. In 1998 he established himself as an art director and marketing consultant, founding two design studios in Seattle, Washington. He has won numerous awards for design.

Thom still visits Interlochen, enjoys Gilbert and Sullivan, and occasionally wears corduroy. He lives in Seattle with his partner, Mike Bergeson, and their cat, Penny.